Reader's Digest

Family Songbook of Faith and Joy

129 All-Time Inspirational Favorites

Editor: William L. Simon

Associates: Nicholas Calabrese   Letitia B. Kehoe   Elizabeth Mead

Music arranged and edited by Dan Fox

Introductions to songs by Clair W. Van Ausdall

The Reader's Digest Association, Inc.
Pleasantville, New York   Montreal

INDEX TO SONGS

Many years ago, one songbook editor's life was brightened by a little girl called Minna. No doubt there was more to her name than that, but theirs was only a brief encounter when he was serving as guest pianist for a Sunday School class in a small Baptist church in the Midwest, and Minna was all he ever knew.

"She was probably about 8 years old," he said. "Blond as butter, small for her age, but stocky, tense with concentration, her face pinched up to its limit in fervor, Minna was singing. And what a singer she was! In a class of perhaps 20, her voice carried easily over the others and out the open window into the October sunlight. Like other children who know totally what they are doing and want you to know that they know, Minna sang louder than anybody else and just a bit ahead of all the others, rushing tempos blissfully, in complete ecstasy.

"The song period of that class went on at some length," he recalled. "Each child got to pick his favorite hymn, and Minna knew them all. She knew every last syllable of every last verse. Finally, when it was her turn to choose, there was no hesitation. Minna selected 'Jesus Wants Me for a Sunbeam' despite the fact that it had been sung just a few minutes before. If she had been singing spiritedly before, now she shouted.

"I will never forget her face, though today, 40 years later, I am not even sure whether she was pretty or plain, only that her pink features were stretched tight with happiness, and she was singing the way children were meant to sing—totally. And she was blind, the victim of a freak accident in her first month of life. Minna had never seen a sunbeam. Perhaps 'never seen' is the wrong way to put it. One look at her face convinced you that she knew exactly what a sunbeam was, and certainly she was *being* a sunbeam—for Him and for all the rest of the world to see."

This book of songs is the kind of book Minna would have wanted, had she been able to read it, not only because it includes that famous Sunday School favorite but because every song herein would give her fresh opportunity to unleash that immense joy in singing.

Over the centuries man has exalted his faith in song. Religion was not always the same for all men, nor is it now. But no matter what we term the center of our belief—Goodness, God, Jehovah, the Divinity of Nature—we surely feel toward it a vast, inexplicable, inexpressible gratitude that somehow can be satisfied by singing. Grandeur in nature, the intimacy of friendship, a personal vision of truth, an unsought gift of healing or comfort, these are manifestations of the ultimate Good that enriches our lives, gives substance to our labor, and promises that love is better than sadness and trust more profitable than greed. And these are things to sing about!

The sheer variety of songs in this book is noteworthy, even for a *Reader's Digest* songbook. They come from all over the world, from so-called classical sources and from popular tunes, from Tin Pan Alley and the Broadway stage, from many denominations of religious belief drawn across many centuries. Doctrinaire is exactly what they are not; rite and particularized creed have no place here. These are expressions of personal feelings, personal identifications with life and the world we live in, personal hopes for the betterment of the world. In all, 129 songs were thoughtfully collected and then appropriately and usefully programmed into 10 large sections.

☆☆☆

Inspirational Hits of the 30's, 40's, and 50's (page 6)
The hard times we knew in every part of the land and in every walk of life in the 30's and the bitter warring that covered the globe in the 40's had the virtue, at least, of showing us what was important; the individual, and his country, and his faith. That return to basic

3

thinking provided the groundswell for a modern renaissance of religion that made itself increasingly apparent in the 50's, as man began once again to care for his spiritual health and not just his economic and intellectual needs. There are lovely songs here—ranging from "I Believe" to "Dear Hearts and Gentle People"—songs of experience and trial and atonement, personal victories, mountain-top inspirations.

☆☆☆

Inspiring Songs From Stage and Screen (page 48)
Composers in Hollywood and on Broadway may be sophisticated musically, but they recognize the tremendous power of simplicity and humble faith as well as anyone. This group of vivid moments from the musical history of the theater, "The Impossible Dream," "Over the Rainbow," "Put On a Happy Face," are by turns tender, exultant, and infectiously lighthearted. Each was the focus for a musical or a film that taught us to think better of ourselves, and to sing while doing it.

☆☆☆

Faith and Joy With a Country Flavor (page 85)
Nowhere do we find today more evidence of confident, satisfying faith than in the leading performers and composers of what we used to call country music. "Country" once meant a few reedy-voiced hill singers living half-forgotten in poor sections of the Deep South. Now, however, with songs like "Stop and Smell the Roses," and "Daddy Sang Bass," all 50 States and many of the lands beyond them are discovering the wholesome pluck, straightforward melodies, and fundamental truths that have characterized for generations the music of close-to-the-soil music lovers and performers in parts of, say, Tennessee and Kentucky. Johnny Cash, Jimmie Davis, and Stuart Hamblen, to name a few, don't consider their songs religious, necessarily; they're simply messages about brotherhood, or what makes the rain fall and the sun shine, or how to ask help from someone who is watching over you.

☆☆☆

An Old-Fashioned Hymn Sing (page 108)
What could be more conducive to good fellowship than this collection of best-loved psalms and gospel tunes of the late 18th and early 19th centuries, when both religious poetry and sacred music reached a pinnacle in craft and communicativeness that we can only call miraculous? No ear can be deaf to the precise beauty of Sarah Fuller Adams' "Nearer, My God, to Thee" (even without the music); no one can deny the vigor of a tune like Simeon Marsh's for "Jesus, Lover of My Soul," which here inspires two entirely separate musical arrangements, by the way—one conventional, the other frankly contemporary in harmony and beat. Beautiful, both.

Sunday School Favorites (page 150)
While hymns like those in the preceding section are sung by adults in churches of every denomination, their youngsters are equally fond of these livelier and, if anything, catchier songs of yesterday and today. One of any song's functions is to teach: Melody helps us all learn, and rhymes fasten good lessons inside our heads easily, securely, and forever. Once you sing "In the Garden" and read the amazing vision that prompted Austin Miles to write it, both tune and story become part of you.

☆☆☆

Popular Hymns of the 60's and 70's (page 173)
Today's relaxed attitudes about so many things, today's clear-eyed discernment of real values, have given us a new and sometimes challenging standard to live up to, but as a reward they have also invested the word Love with fresh meaning. Today's songs don't rhyme June and moon and spoon very much, but tell us instead of love for each other as brothers, love of the good things around us, love of contentment, love of love. Such songs make you want to join in, first of all—who can resist the magic of "I'd Like To Teach the World To Sing"?—but they also make you thoughtful and thankful.

☆☆☆

Favorites of the Folk Singers (page 206)
Balladeers have been coming on stronger and stronger ever since the late 1930's, when musical pioneers like Pete Seeger and Woody Guthrie began to show us the treasures that lay in our native song. Nowadays many folk artists write their own bits of treasure in that same rugged, appealing, individualistic style, but with one important difference: They can sing their songs to national popularity in a matter of months. Musical Americana is being created right around us, and this section presents a group of special attractiveness because the songs, such as "Turn! Turn! Turn!" and "If I Had a Hammer," concern justice, fellowship, and peace for all men.

☆☆☆

Best Loved Spirituals (page 223)
It was Anton Dvořák, famous Czech composer of the "Symphony From the New World" among many other masterpieces, who on an extended visit to this country discovered our Negro spirituals and marveled at them: "They are a product of your soil. They are purely American; they are the true folk song of America." Others since have called spirituals the finest distinctive artistic contribution America has to offer the world. No longer are they only the eloquent musical speech of black people in bondage. They have become the heritage of all Americans. Some sing of strength for this world, to be rewarded by grace in the next, across the

great river. Some, like "Were You There?" can make you weep with their lyricism and intimacy. Some can make you smile as you recognize that age-old fallibilities are not black or white, but human.

☆☆☆

Songs To Follow the Sunset (page 242)
Glorious as the daylight is, a particular mellowness settles over the land at twilight, and the songs commemorating the hours when rest is near at hand and work is thankfully laid by are as sweet as sleep itself—"Brahms' Lullaby," "Sweet Hour of Prayer," "May the Good Lord Bless and Keep You," for example. Sing them as lullabys, use them as farewells, repeat them as comforting alleluias at the sunset of a happy day or a richly blessed life.

☆☆☆

"That's America to Me!" (page 271)
If you read the short paragraphs that precede each song in this final section, you will see that almost every one of the songs was inspired by some splendor of nature or some highly charged event that could only have happened in the America we so much love to sing about. Notice, for example, that all the stanzas for Katherine Lee Bates' "America the Beautiful" are included—it's a panoramic, richly detailed picture of the grandeur of our homeland that should make all Americans realize anew, each time we read it, how blessed we are.

All are superb songs, we know you'll agree, just waiting here to be sung and sung again and again. Their arrangements are one of the finest aspects of the book, each of them done by Dan Fox with a skill and originality that borders on genius. You can enjoy them in lots of ways. Basically, of course, they are vocal lines with a piano accompaniment, always interesting, yet easy to play for the average pianist, and possible even for the musician of the most modest attainments. The melody line (with stems turned up) may also be played by a solo treble-clef C-instrument, including violin, flute, recorder, oboe, and harmonica. Guitar diagrams above the staves make the guitarist's life easy, and the small notes in the bass line (with stems turned down) show an organist an adequate pedal part for any instrument, small or large. Accordionists can play the melody with their right hands and produce on-the-spot accompaniments by using the chord symbols for their left-hand buttons. Bass players, either string or brass, can play along by using the small notes in the bass clef or by heeding the chord symbols. Practically any combination of instruments is possible, and any addition is welcome.

Most of the arrangements are just two pages long, so that the number of page turns within any song has been held to an absolute minimum. A few songs may be familiar to you from the other *Reader's Digest* songbooks. They were just too perfectly suited to the spirit of this one to omit; so they appear again but with entirely new and different arrangements.

Not long ago, one of our associates joined a few members of his family for a day's reunion in central Iowa. During evening dinner they carried on the fevered conversation that had broken out as they all arrived in the afternoon, but in the slight lull that followed someone suggested a bit of music. "I was the first to 'oblige,' as we used to term these dutiful family performances years ago, with some pieces by Rachmaninoff and Chopin," our colleague told us. "But it was not until my uncle said, 'Come on, Floy, play some of the old hymns,' and my 83-year-old mother, to this day a church organist after a lifetime in music, sat down to the same keyboard and began to sail into such favorites as 'How Great Thou Art' and 'Abide With Me' that the room came alive with music. From my uncle, aged 81, to a 13-year-old cousin whose voice was changing, and with 18 or 20 others at various ages in between, they were all singing along, totally, and in total pleasure. I thought then, wouldn't the songbook we've been working on be a priceless treasure for just this kind of gathering! Who knows? Had we had a copy that evening we might still be there, all of us together, picking our favorites, remembering long-forgotten stanzas, and trying to outsing each other for the sheer joy of it."

—THE EDITORS

I Believe

Jane Froman, preparing a television show in 1952, one day happened to see a letter from a serviceman then in Korea. She and her team of writers, particularly Ervin Drake who later recalled the incident, created "I Believe" as their reply to him and to everyone seeking a way to put honest basic faith into words. This was a "song that would give the average person hope," Drake said. Miss Froman's performance on the show "USA Canteen" was a great success, and the following year Frankie Laine's recording sold a million copies. As a result, he used the music practically as a theme song. Hit Parade analysts named "I Believe" the most successful song of 1953, and it won the Christophers' award as the finest inspirational tune of the year.

Words and Music by Ervin Drake, Irvin Graham, Jimmy Shirl, and Al Stillman

TRO – © Copyright 1952 & 1953 CROMWELL MUSIC, INC., New York, N.Y. Used by Permission.

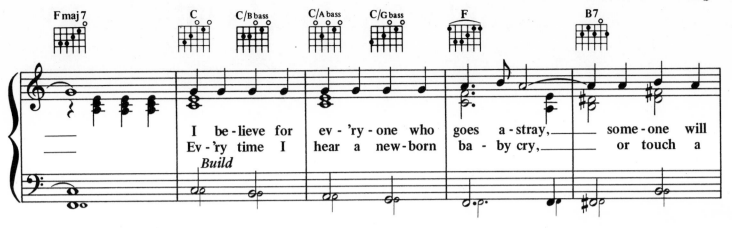

I be-lieve for ev-'ry-one who goes a-stray,_____ some-one will
Ev-'ry time I hear a new-born ba-by cry,_____ or touch a
Build

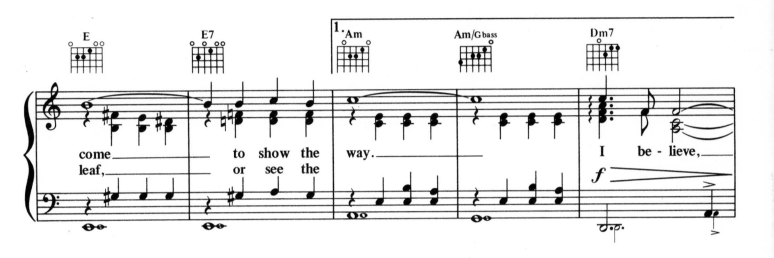

come_____ I be-lieve,_____
leaf,_____ to show the way._____ *f*
or see the

I be-lieve.
sky,_____ then I know

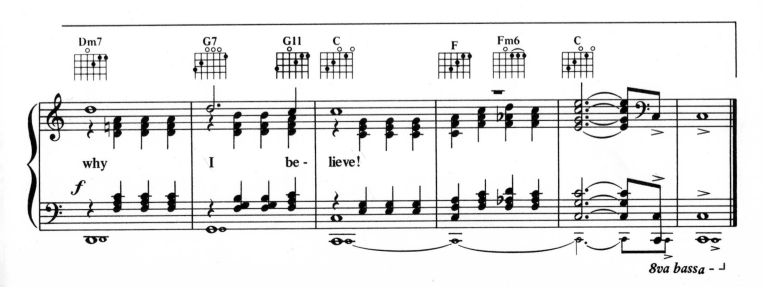

why I be-lieve!
f

8va bassa - ┘

Dear Hearts and Gentle People

America's beloved ballad writer Stephen Foster died alone and in poverty, having squandered his magnificent talent (and such money as he made from it) on drink. In the jacket pocket of his shabby suit was found a scrap of paper with the phrase "Dear hearts and gentle people," perhaps the beginning of another imperishable Foster song like "Beautiful Dreamer" or "My Old Kentucky Home." The words appealed to Bob Hilliard so much when he heard of them in 1949 that he continued the lyrics, and Sammy Fain, who had already won Academy Awards for such tunes as "Love Is a Many-Splendored Thing" and "Secret Love," furnished the music for this song. Dinah Shore and Bing Crosby vied for top honors among a long list of successful recording artists.

Words by Bob Hilliard   Music by Sammy Fain

nev - er ev - er   let   you   down._____ They read the
pick - et fence and ram - bling

rose._____

_____ I feel so wel - come   each time that I re - turn that my

hap - py heart keeps laugh - ing like a   clown._____ I love the

dear   hearts   and   gen - tle   peo - ple   who

live and love   in   my home - town._____   _ff_

9

How Great Thou Art

It was an English missionary named Stuart K. Hine who brought "How Great Thou Art" to the attention of the world after he heard it on his travels through the Ukraine in the 1930's. His conjecture was that the song, originally attributed to a Swedish divine, Carl Boberg, found its way there in the repertoire of traveling penitents who sang pious anthems as they wandered from place to place. Hine translated the text and notated the music from memory; both resemble to some degree a sacred song, "The Almighty," written nearly a century earlier by Franz Schubert. "How Great Thou Art" has become universally familiar and beloved mainly because of its being a part of Billy Graham's Crusade music; more than 150 recorded versions existed as of 1974, in an extraordinary range of devotional styles.

English words by Stuart K. Hine

(1) O Lord my God! When I in awe-some won-der ___ Con-sid-er all the worlds Thy hands have made; ___ I see the stars, I hear the roll-ing

(2) When through the woods and for-est glades I wan-der ___ And hear the birds sing sweet-ly in the trees; ___ When I look down from loft-y moun-tain

(3) And when I think that God, His Son not spar-ing, ___ Sent Him to die, I scarce can take it in; ___ That on the cross my bur-den glad-ly

(4) When Christ shall come with shout of ac-cla-ma-tion ___ And take me home, what joy shall fill my heart! ___ Then I shall bow in hum-ble a-do-

11

Somebody Bigger Than You and I

The words for this song were written on the back of a golf card in 1951, recalls lyricist Johnny Lange. Golfing with friends, he suddenly became intensely aware of the beautiful California day — the incredibly blue skies overhead, the purple shadows on the mountains in the distance, the vast stretches of golden sand — and began to jot short phrases on his scorecard: "Who made the

mountain," "Who made the river. . . ." The song wrote itself, he says. For a title he used a phrase remembered from his childhood, a favorite expression of his father, from whom he derived his abiding love of nature. A few days later the music was completed as well. Over the years this song has been performed in the White House for three Presidents.

Words and Music by Johnny Lange, Hy Heath, and Sonny Burke

Who made the moun-tain, who made the tree, Who made the riv-er
Who makes the flow-ers, bloom in the spring, Who writes the song for the

flow to the sea, And who hung the moon in the star-ry sky?
rob-in to sing, And who sends the rain when the earth is dry?

Some-bod-y big-ger than you and I.
you and I.___ He lights the way when the

Crying in the Chapel

It must have been a proud moment for Artie Glenn in 1953 when he heard his son Darrell introduce this song that he had just written. Soon after, such varying interpretations as those of June Valli, Rex Allen, and The Orioles all became eminently successful recordings, and in 1965 the song became a million-seller for Elvis Presley.

Words and Music by Artie Glenn

You saw me cry-ing in the
(Ev-'ry sin-ner looks for)

chap - el,_____ The tears I shed were tears of joy;_____
some - thing_____ That will put his heart at ease;_____

_____ I know the mean-ing of con - tent - ment,_____ Now I am hap - py with the
There is on - ly one true an - swer,_____ He must get down on his

If I Can Help Somebody

The Arizona composer Alma Bazel Androzzo was living in Chicago when she wrote her best known inspirational song, "If I Can Help Somebody." It was published there and might have achieved only modest success had it not been for some servicemen who brought it to England at the end of World War II and sang it there. Ralph Boosey, the famous music publisher, heard it, secured the rights to it, and helped make the song an international hit. A few of the varied and particularly compelling recorded versions are those of Gracie Fields, the English vaudeville star; George "Bev" Shea, soloist with Billy Graham; Tennessee Ernie Ford; Doris Day; Mahalia Jackson; Billy Eckstine; and the duet version by Dale Evans and Roy Rogers.

Words and Music by A. Bazel Androzzo

word or song, If I can show some -
world up wrought, If I can spread love's

bod - y he is trav - 'ling wrong,
mes - sage that the Mas - ter taught, Then my

liv - ing shall not be in vain.

REFRAIN

Then my liv - ing shall not be in vain,

18

The Man Upstairs

In 1954 Dorinda Morgan, Harold Stanley, and Gerry Manners collaborated on a song with lots of deep-down conviction about "the Man upstairs" and how He can be relied upon for hope and comfort, no matter how badly all the weak souls "downstairs" manage to tangle up their lives. A best-selling recording of the song was done country-style by the four Stanley Brothers (no relation to Harold). After their version had become a hit, two of the brothers were killed in a tragic airplane accident, and the remaining two sang this song at the funeral service.

Words and Music by Dorinda Morgan, Harold Stanley, and Gerry Manners

Moderate gospel tempo (with a swing)

Have you talked to the Man up-stairs, 'Cause He wants to hear from you, Have you talked to the Man up-stairs, He will al-ways see you thru. And if trou-ble ev-er trou-bles you, Don't you run and hide, 'Cause if

you ev-er need a friend, He'll be right there by your side. Just

turn your eyes t'ward heav-en, and say a sim-ple pray'r, Thru clouds of lace you'll

see His face, No mat-ter when or where. Have you talked to the Man up-

Hold back a little　　*In tempo*

N.C.

stairs, He wants to hear from you. Have you talked to the Man up-

G7 C G C D G B7

Em A7 D7 G C7 G7

Cadenza—freely

stairs, He will al-ways see you thru.

Suddenly There's a Valley

Mountaintop experiences give drama to our spiritual lives, but we look to the valleys between them for comfort and serenity in our day-to-day living. In the Old Testament we are told that "Every valley shall be lifted up," and throughout the centuries since, valleys have represented a life of quietude and protection from the storms of crisis. Pianist Chuck Meyer and actor Biff Jones wrote this song in 1955, emphasizing its gentle calmness by setting it to a fluid ¾ beat. It provided bestselling records for both Gogi Grant and Jo Stafford.

Words and Music by Chuck Meyer and Biff Jones

When you've climbed the
(When a) storm hides the

high-est moun-tain,
dis-tant rain-bow

When a cloud holds the sun-shine in,
And you think you can't find a friend,

Sud-den-ly there's a val-ley
Sud-den-ly there's a val-ley

Where the earth knows
Where the friend-ships

peace with man.
nev-er

When a

end.

Touched on-ly

I Heard a Forest Praying

In 1937 popular songwriter Peter De Rose (whose famous tunes include "Deep Purple") composed a musical setting for a poem by Sam M. Lewis. De Rose divided the four stanzas into three sections: "The Dream," "The Prayer," and "The Awakening." These divisions point out the contrast between the inherent nobility of trees and the heartbreaking uses man makes of them—a tree was the cross for the Son of Man; forests are made into battlefields. (Interestingly enough, De Rose was later to compose a musical setting for a distinctly militaristic poem by Gen. George S. Patton, Jr.) "I Heard a Forest Praying" was unique among De Rose's songs, which were mostly romantic ballads. He and his wife, May Singhi Breen, used to sing his romantic songs on their radio show in the 1920's and 1930's, a show that earned them the sobriquet of "The Sweethearts of the Air."

Words by Sam M. Lewis   Music by Peter De Rose

One Little Candle

Portia, in Shakespeare's The Merchant of Venice, *points out that one burning candle stands out like a good deed in a world of wickedness. And the motto of the Christopher society, which inspired this song, expresses almost the same thought: "It is better to light one candle than to curse the darkness." Both J. Maloy Roach and George Mysels, the writers of "One Little Candle," lit their own candles, so to speak, during World War II, when they gave unceasingly of their talent in performing at USO's and military bases. "One Little Candle" is their best known collaboration, particularly because of Perry Como's hit recording of the song in 1952.*

Words and Music by J. Maloy Roach and George Mysels

Take My Hand, Precious Lord

This, the most famous of Thomas A. Dorsey's many devotional songs, was born of sorrow. Death had robbed Dorsey of both his wife and his young child, and for many months his anguish was almost overpowering. Then one night he attended an inspirational meeting with friends, *and as he lay sleepless afterward the words "Take my hand..." began to form themselves in his mind, "almost," he says, "like drops of water falling into a deep, calm pool." Both the lyrics and music of the song are rooted in the Negro spiritual, and its message is universal.*

Words and Music by Thomas A. Dorsey

His Name Is Wonderful

Audrey Mieir and her husband, both ordained ministers, were sharing the pastorate of a small California church with his brother and his wife in 1956. On Christmas Day she sat among her young people's choir as her brother-in-law began his sermon with a paraphrase of the joyous and prophetic verse from Isaiah 9:6: "His name will be called Wonderful." So moved by the sermon, by the love that surrounded her on the faces of the children and their parents, and by the spirit of Christmas that seemed almost tangible, she wrote a poem and its melody (on the flyleaf of a Bible) in a matter of minutes. Some years later, when Mrs. Mieir and her husband arrived in the Orient as missionaries to the "nameless children" born during the Korean War, they found that this song had preceded them and was being sung by the people they had come to serve.

Words and Music by Audrey Mieir

HE

With a simple pronoun Richard Mullan suggested the all-powerful Supreme Being who is slow to anger and quick to solace at the same time. Jack Richards' music for this song completed the mood. The lofty, melodious song proved ideal for singer Al Hibbler in 1954, and his recording was a bestseller.

Words by Richard Mullan
Music by Jack Richards

*Play chords finger style.

My Cathedral

(The Home I Love)

Just as every man's home is his castle, so every man's heart is his cathedral. Wherever your own source of gratitude and memory and love lies, there your chapel stands, ready to receive you in prayer. Hal Eddy's lyrics echo a poem by Thomas Hood written almost exactly a century earlier. To Hood, "Each cloud-capped mountain is a holy altar;/ An organ breathes in every grove." Mabel Wayne, whose long songwriting career is studded with hits like "Ramona" and "It Happened in Monterey," provided the music.

Words by Hal Eddy   Music by Mabel Wayne

My ca-the-dral is a sim-ple place, Built of mem-'ries and glad-ness and tears, And it's here I find real peace in my heart, And it's here I've pray'd for years. It has no choir__ soft-ly

Whither Thou Goest

Words and Music by Guy Singer

Guy Singer based his lyrics for this quiet song on the Old Testament story of Ruth and Naomi, in which Ruth, the daughter-in-law, pledges her fidelity to the mother of her dead husband. Many settings of her famous words have been made, including one done especially for the marriage of Elizabeth II to Prince Philip. But none is more appropriate to the trusting mood of the text than this one, which was beautifully interpreted by Les Paul and Mary Ford in their bestselling disc of 1954.

Bluebird of Happiness

Jan Peerce, who introduced Edward Heyman and San-dor Harmati's "Bluebird of Happiness," was for many years one of the leading tenors at the Metropolitan Opera in New York — and possibly the only one who began his career on the so-called borscht circuit as a violinist and bandleader. Later he starred for nearly 10 years at the then new Radio City Music Hall before moving on to the Met for an operatic career that spanned more than 20 years. All the time he was adding to his collection of bird figurines, inspired originally by this song and his extraordinary success with it. In 1948 Art Mooney and his orchestra recorded another version that sold a million copies.

Words by Edward Heyman   Music by Sandor Harmati

REFRAIN

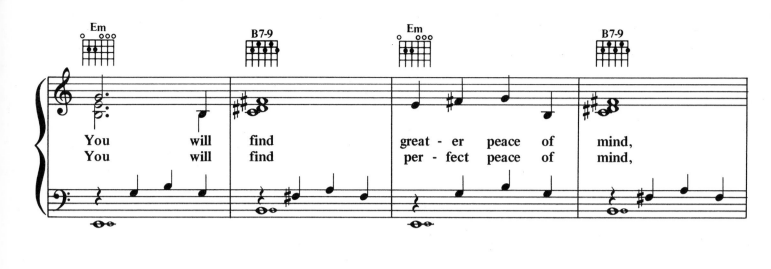

You will find greater peace of mind,
You will find perfect peace of mind,

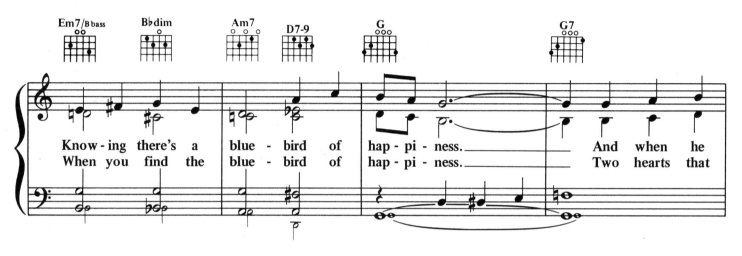

Know-ing there's a blue-bird of hap-pi-ness. And when he
When you find the blue-bird of hap-pi-ness. Two hearts that

sings to you, Though you're deep in blue,
beat as one 'Neath a new-found sun,

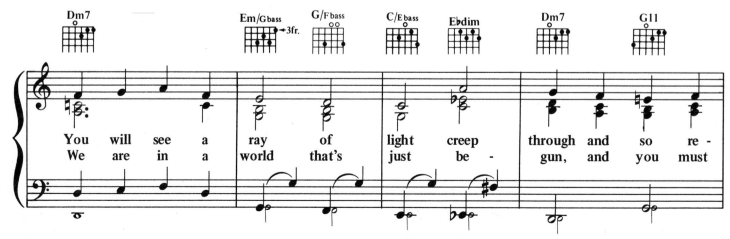

You will see a ray of light creep through and so re-
We are in a world that's just be-gun, and you must

40

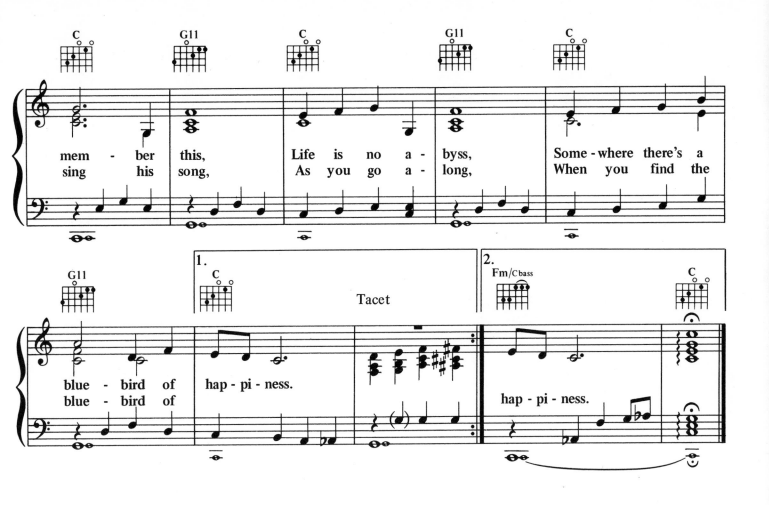

mem - ber this,
sing - his song,

Life is no a - byss,
As you go a - long,

Some - where there's a
When you find the

blue - bird of hap - pi - ness.
blue - bird of

hap - pi - ness.

Recitation for "Bluebird of Happiness"

as recorded by Jan Peerce

The poet with his pen,
The peasant with his plough,
It makes no difference who you are,
It's all the same somehow.

The king upon his throne,
The jester at his feet,
The artist, the actress, the man on the street—
It's a life of smiles
And a life of tears,
It's a life of hopes
And a life of fears.
A blinding torrent of rain
And a brilliant burst of sun,
A biting, tearing pain
And bubbling, sparkling fun—
And no matter what you have,
Don't envy those you meet;
It's all the same, it's in the game,
The bitter and the sweet.
And if things don't look so cheerful,
Just show a little fight,
For every bit of darkness
There's a little bit of light.

For every bit of hatred
There's a little bit of love,
For every cloudy morning
There's a midnight moon above!

No Man Is an Island

The great English poet and parson John Donne (1573–1631) is revered today as much for his sermons as for his poems, and from one of the former comes the marvelous passage that ends: "And therefore, never send to know for whom the bell tolls; it tolls for thee." This same passage, which gave Ernest Hemingway the title for his famous novel, begins with, "No man is an island, entire of itself; every man is a piece of the continent, a part of the main," the text that Joan Whitney and Alex Kramer paraphrased for this lovely song written in 1950.

Words and Music by Joan Whitney and Alex Kramer

No man is an is-land, No man stands a-lone,

Each man's joy is joy to me, Each man's grief is my own.

Anyone Can Move a Mountain

Johnny Marks, a Phi Beta Kappa member, wrote "Rudolph the Red-Nosed Reindeer," one of the most popular secular Christmas songs since he dashed it off in 1949. In 1966 he combined philosophy with musical adroitness in "Anyone Can Move a Mountain," written for the television spectacular "Ballad of Smokey the Bear." Lawrence Welk lists this uplifting song as one of his favorites and often features it on his show.

Words and Music by Johnny Marks

An-y-one can move a moun-tain if he real-ly tries.

An-y-one can move a moun-tain, you must re-al-ize.

It will take a lit-tle time, a lot of faith, make up your mind, and

I May Never Pass This Way Again

"If I can . . . help one fainting Robin/Unto his Nest again/I shall not live in Vain," wrote the American poet Emily Dickinson in 1858. Almost exactly 100 years later two contemporary lyricists, Murray Wizell and Irving Melsher, put the same positive sentiment of charity and fulfillment into a country song, writing their own music as well. The song proved once again that there is a special compatibility between country tunes and deep-down gospel truths.

Words and Music by Murray Wizell and Irving Melsher

The Impossible Dream

From *Man of La Mancha*

"Only he who attempts the ridiculous may achieve the impossible." This epigram from a Spanish writer inspired television author Dale Wasserman to do a play about another Spanish writer, Miguel de Cervantes, and his most famous literary creation, Don Quixote, the Man of La Mancha. It was particularly responsible, he says, for the show's pivotal song, "The Impossible Dream," known also as "The Quest." Mitch Leigh, formerly a jingle writer, composed the music for the show, whose staged version opened in a small renovated opera house on the banks of the Connecticut River. Finally, having struggled to an Off-Broadway house in New York, *Man of La Mancha achieved its rightful reception, transferring to Broadway as well as to practically every metropolitan center in the world. Richard Kiley, playing the old and frail Don Quixote who lives nobly because his vision is noble, made an irradicable impression on every audience with this operatic song.*

Words by Joe Darion   Music by Mitch Leigh

*Each bar of $\frac{9}{8}$ time should be felt as three slow beats: 1 2 3 4 5 6 7 8 9

bear_____ with un - bear - a - ble sor - row,_____ to
try_____ when your arms are too wea - ry,_____ to

1. run_____ where the brave dare not go._____ To

2. reach_____ the un - reach - a - ble star! This is my

quest,_____ to fol - low that star,_____ No mat - ter how

hope - less,_____ no mat - ter how far; _____ To fight for the

right _____ with-out ques-tion or pause, _____ To be will-ing to march in-to hell for a heav-en-ly cause! And I know, _____ if I'll on-ly be true _____ To this glo-ri-ous quest _____ that my heart _____ will lie peace-ful and calm, _____ When I'm laid to my rest.

Hold back a little

And the

50

world_____ will be bet - ter for this;_____ That one

man,_____ scorned and cov - ered with scars,_____ still___

strove_____ with his last ounce of cour - age,_____ To

Slowing down

reach_____ the un - reach - a - ble stars._____

In tempo

Oh, What a Beautiful Mornin'

From *Oklahoma!*

No Broadway musical had ever started with a stage empty of people except for one old woman churning butter. But then, until Okla-homa! came along in 1943, no musical had ever started with a song like "Oh, What a Beautiful Mornin'," which the hero, Curly, begins from offstage. Its warmth and sheer delight in the glories of nature on a fine day waltzed each evening's show off to a magical beginning for 5 years and 9 weeks. Hammerstein worked for 3 weeks on the lyrics to create "an atmosphere of relaxation and ten-derness." Rodgers, on the other hand, dashed off the melody in about 10 minutes. No matter; the effect was perfection.

Words by Oscar Hammerstein II   Music by Richard Rodgers

Look for the Silver Lining

From *Sally*

Florenz Ziegfeld, who always knew when he had a great star in orbit, asked Jerome Kern to do a special song for the blonde beauty who was going to have top billing in his 1920 production, Sally. Kern and his lyricist, Buddy DeSylva, gave him one they had written previously and liked a lot — "Look for the Silver Lining." *It turned out to be the hit of the show and perfect for the charming Marilyn Miller. Miss Miller, of course, went on to become her own kind of legend. And when a film biography was made of her life in 1949, "Look for the Silver Lining" provided the title.*

Words by Buddy DeSylva   Music by Jerome Kern

55

DAY BY DAY

From *Godspell*

Contemporary though it is, Godspell, the fresh-as-tomorrow off-Broadway combination of rock music and the New Testament story of Jesus, goes back to some old sources. The name, for one thing, is the ancient spelling of our word "gospel," meaning "good news." For another, "Day by Day," its most popular song, is based on words attributed to an English saint and bishop of the mid-13th century, Richard of Chichester. He, it is thought, had modeled his short meditation on the simple and compelling three prayers handed down from St. Francis of Assisi.

Words and Music by Stephen Schwartz

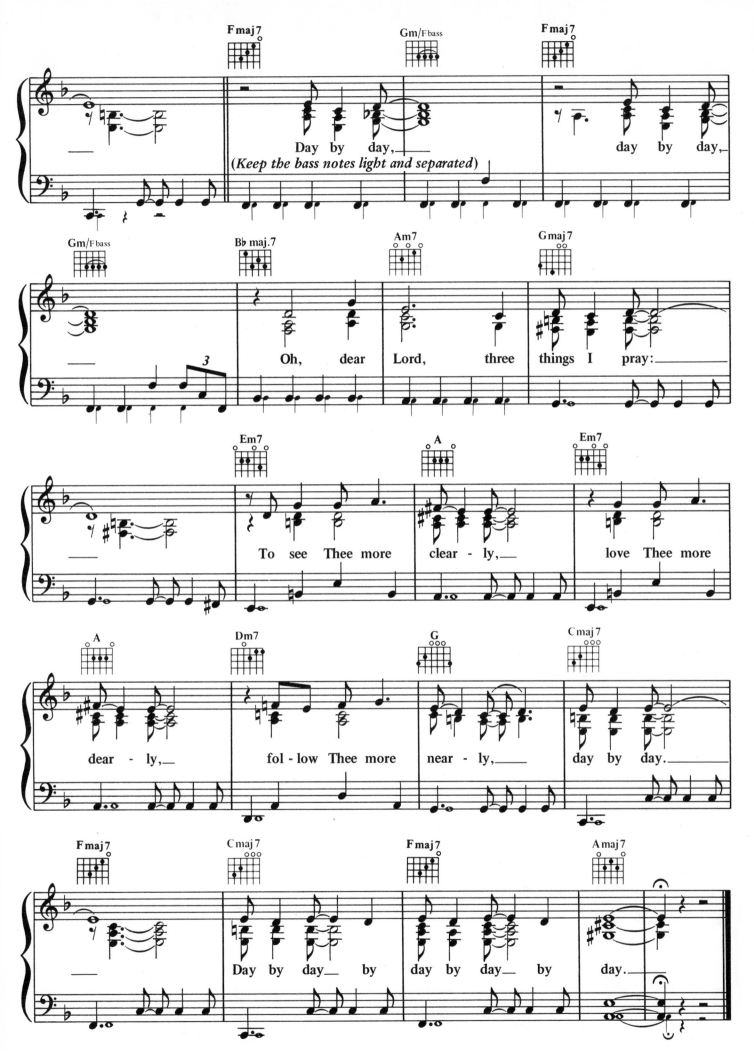

Put On a Happy Face

From Bye Bye Birdie

There was once a most ill-tempered man who was persuaded by his neighbors to wear a mask with a smile on it. He wore the mask so long that when it accidentally broke, the townspeople discovered that the man was smiling all by himself. That same message, more or less, is the good advice of "Put On a Happy Face," *a song from the frantically paced 1960 Broadway musical* Bye Bye Birdie, *which made stars of Dick Van Dyke, Chita Rivera, and Paul Lynde, while it good-heartedly spoofed the whole rock-and-roll era and the cult of Youth for Youth's Sake.*

Words by Lee Adams   Music by Charles Strouse

58

The Sound of Music

From *The Sound of Music*

The film version of Rodgers and Hammerstein's The Sound of Music *opened with a shot of Julie Andrews, in the vivid springtime of the majestic Austrian Alps, singing "The hills are alive...." It was an exaltation of nature, of love for life, of fulfillment in joy, and it still crowns the score of this prize-winning, record-breaking musical that had dazzled Broadway with* Mary Martin *just as it was later to dazzle Hollywood and all the world with Miss Andrews. Both stage and screen versions of* The Sound of Music *radiated the charm and wholesomeness so characteristic of the famous composer-lyricist team. Rodgers himself once remarked, "What's wrong with sweetness and light? They've been around quite a while!"*

Words by Oscar Hammerstein II   Music by Richard Rodgers

Climb Ev'ry Mountain

From *The Sound of Music*

Maria, the high-spirited postulant, has been sent out from her Austrian abbey to serve temporarily as governess to the children of Captain von Trapp. Dismayed that she has fallen in love with the captain, Maria flees back to the abbey. There the Mother Abbess assures her that the love of a man and woman is holy and that she must reach out to grasp the good things in life. . . . It happened, of course, in The Sound of Music. The Abbess' advice was tendered in this noble song. "Climb Ev'ry Mountain" resounds once more at the end of the play when the Trapps, helped by the abbey nuns, elude their Nazi pursuers and make their way over the mountain—to freedom.

Words by Oscar Hammerstein II   Music by Richard Rodgers

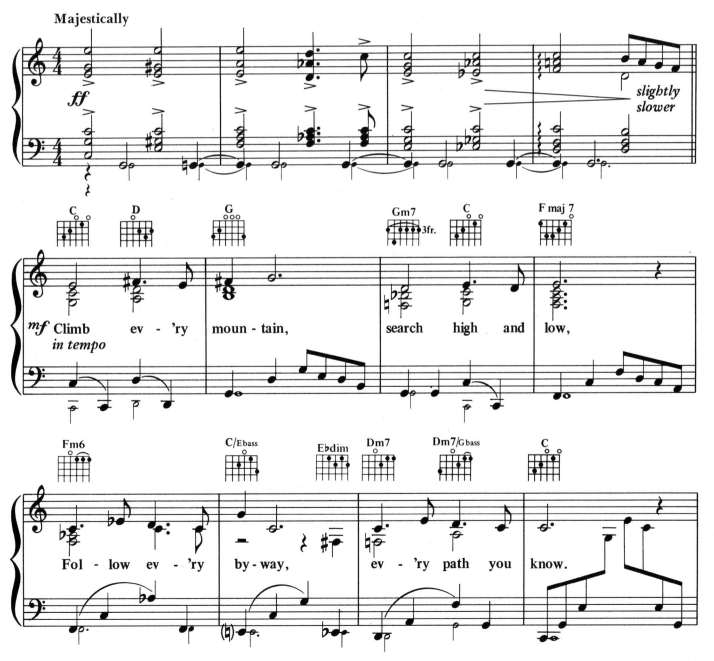

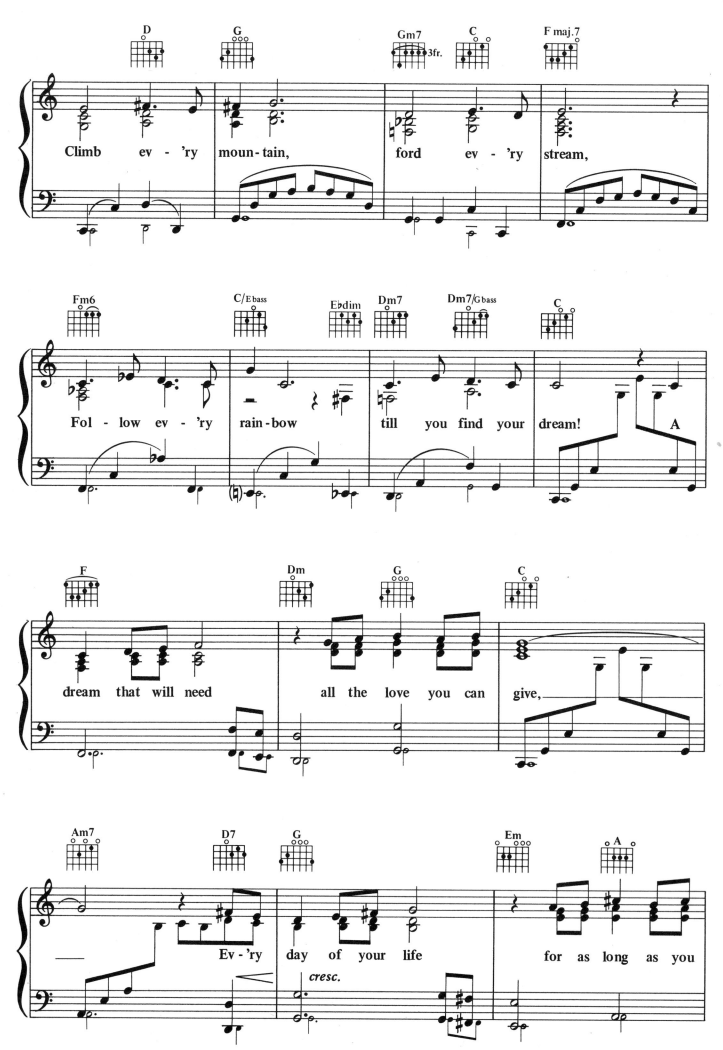

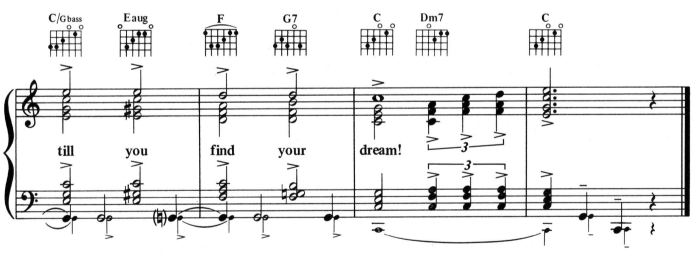

The Best Things in Life Are Free

From *Good News*

Good News was perhaps the most successful of a spate of college shows that radiated energy, youth, and football in the mid-1920's. "The Varsity Drag," one of the musical's big hits, was all rah-rah rhythm and vitality; the other, "The Best Things in Life Are Free," was a sweet, tender duet in which a rich boy told his not-so-rich sweetheart that money didn't really matter. What was important then, as well as now, was something like the Moon, the Sun, the stars, or, best of all, love — the things that belong to everyone and make life worthwhile.

**Words and Music by B. G. DeSylva,
Lew Brown, and Ray Henderson**

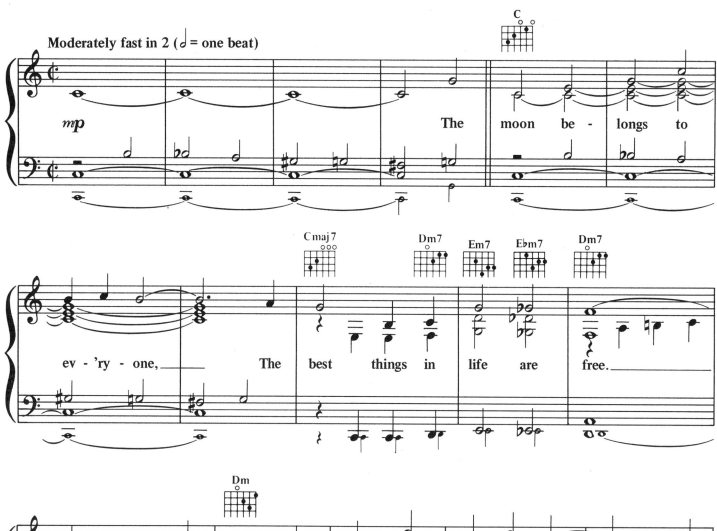

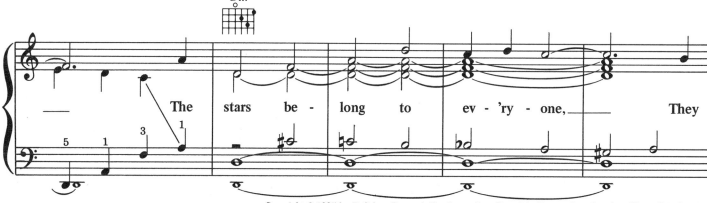

SMILE

From *Modern Times*

To win his reputation as the cinema's most gifted personality, Charlie Chaplin, the beguiling "little tramp" of Hollywood's golden days, used as one of his trademarks a shy, winsome, fleeting, little smile. Chaplin became much more than just a star actor, however. By 1936 when he was at work on his masterpiece, Modern Times, he had become author, director, set designer, and musical director as well. The theme music he composed for the film quite naturally was called "Smile." Lyrics were not added until 1954, and even today the tune is best known as an instrumental.

Words by John Turner and Geoffrey Parsons   Music by Charles Chaplin

Look to the Rainbow

From *Finian's Rainbow*

Finian's Rainbow, a fantastic combination of Irish leprechauns and American sharecroppers, first shone on Broadway in 1947. No show ever generated more rainbows. One is Rainbow Valley, the mythical town in which the story takes place; another is the one Finian hopes to make in reverse by planting a crock of gold he has brought from the auld sod; the third is the number that always stopped the show — "Look to the Rainbow." Actress Ella Logan, who played the heroine of the show as if she had been born an Irish colleen, always buttered the lyrics liberally with her beautiful brogue, and the song became indelibly associated with her.

Words by E. Y. Harburg   Music by Burton Lane

OVER THE RAINBOW

From *The Wizard of Oz*

Judy Garland . . . "Over the Rainbow" . . . Some stars find their theme songs early, and Judy Garland discovered hers as a child star in The Wizard of Oz, that Hollywood classic released in 1939. The song won the Academy Award that year, though it had been cut from the film on at least three occasions because it seemed too slow, too time consuming. At the last minute it was reinstated and became the high point of one of the finest movie scores ever composed. Originally Harold Arlen intended his tune to be sonorous and imposingly grand, but E. Y. Harburg, who was to write the lyrics for it, said, "That's for Nelson Eddy, not a little girl in Kansas." With a simplified texture and harmony, the tune became absolutely perfect for Dorothy, as played by Judy Garland. Needless to say, Garland fans could never get enough of the song; as long as she sang, "Over the Rainbow" was as much Judy Garland herself as those immense brown eyes and that vulnerable smile.

Words by E. Y. Harburg   Music by Harold Arlen

74

Make Someone Happy

From *Do Re Mi*

The jukebox business and the invasion into the music world by gangsters were at the center of Garson Kanin's musical *Do Re Mi*, which first appeared on Broadway in 1960. The prevailing mood was blustery humor, but on the softer side came the philosophical song "Make Someone Happy," with words based on the old Sunday School proverb: "To be happy, you must first make others happy." With a tune by Jule Styne, this Broadway version is more charming than the words alone.

Words by Betty Comden and Adolph Green   Music by Jule Styne

D.C. and fade out on Introduction

SUNRISE, SUNSET

From *Fiddler on the Roof*

Fiddler on the Roof *became the longest running musical in Broadway history—it ran from September 1964 to July 1972—even though it took a sober look at downtrodden Jews managing a precarious existence in a poor Russian village circa 1905. What made such long-lasting joy in the theater were the staunch beauty of family life, even in such circumstances, and the traditions and courage that supported it. Based on stories by Sholom Aleichem, the show starred Zero Mostel and Maria Karnilova. As the play unfolds, they suddenly realize the fleetness of time's passing, and they sing the haunting* "Sunrise, Sunset." *The song's somber beauty stood out even in a score that included* "Matchmaker, Matchmaker" *and* "If I Were a Rich Man."

Words by Sheldon Harnick   Music by Jerry Bock

80

Sun - rise, sun - set, sun - rise, sun - set,

Swift - ly fly the years;

One sea - son fol - low - ing an - oth - er,

Lad - en with hap - pi - ness and tears.

2nd time, softer and softer to the end

ppp

8va bassa

You'll Never Walk Alone

From *Carousel*

Carousel, *Rodgers and Hammerstein's musical about life in rural New England, is a story of happiness and sadness, of strength and weakness. The heroine, Julie, loves the irresponsible, happy-go-lucky, smooth-talking carnival barker, Billy. That much is happy. But when Billy tries for some easy money, and then kills himself rather than be caught, Julie is overwhelmed in tears until her friend Nettie offers her some of the most beautiful comfort ever written in a song in "You'll Never Walk Alone." This modern-day anthem of trust, embraced by all religions and loved by all the world ever since 1945, has a new spirituality and an increased dramatic intensity that immediately distinguishes it from the songs Rodgers had written up to that time. Dorothy Rodgers, the composer's wife, lists this as one of her four top favorites among his work.*

Words by Oscar Hammerstein II   Music by Richard Rodgers

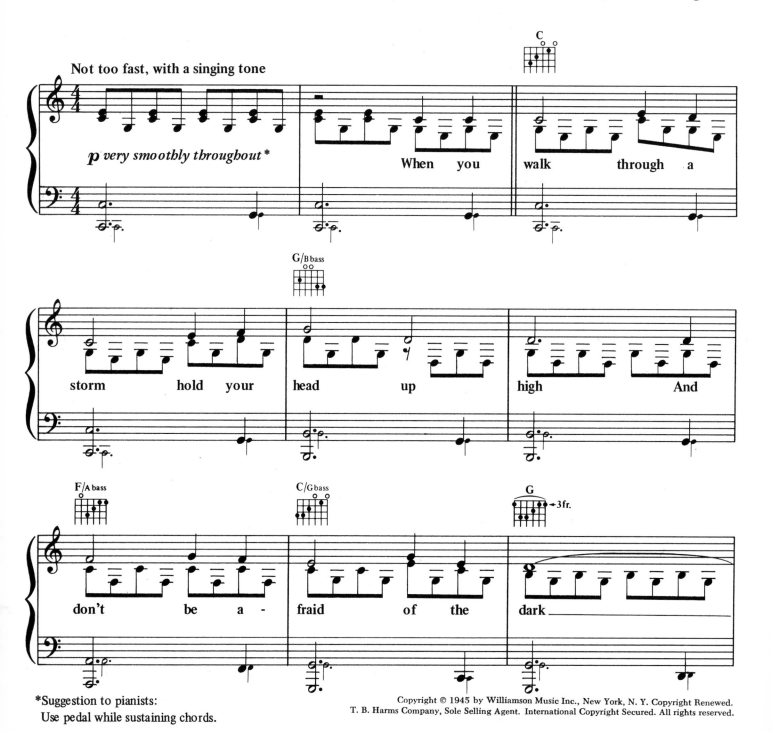

*Suggestion to pianists:
  Use pedal while sustaining chords.

Stop and Smell the Roses

Country singer Mac Davis set to music his own beliefs, and the song became an outstanding hit of 1974. His collaborator was Doc Severinsen, bandleader for a popular television talk show on which Davis, a frequent guest, effortlessly tells anecdotes from the life of "a traveling singer-man," which is what he terms himself. Mentioning the line of the lyrics that goes, "Did you kiss your wife and tell her that she's pretty," the host of the show once asked Davis if he followed his own advice. "You bet," was the reply. "Every day!"

Words and Music by Mac Davis and Doc Severinsen

85

(1) Hey, mis - ter, where you go - in' in such a hur - ry?____
(2) Be - fore you went to work this morn - in' in the cit - y____
(3) Did you ev - er take a walk thru the for - est?____

(1) Well, don't you think it's time you re - al - ized there's a
(2) Did you spend some time with the fam' - ly? Did you
(3) Stop and dream a - while a - mong the trees? You can

(1) whole lot more to life____ than work and wor - ry?____ The
(2) kiss your wife and tell____ her that she's pret - ty?____ Did you
(3) look up thru the leaves____ right straight to heav - en____ and you can

(1) sweet - est things in life are free____ and they're right be - fore your eyes.____ But you got to
(2) take your chil - dren to your breast____ and love 'em ten - der - ly?____ You got to
(3) al - most hear the voice of God____ in each and ev - 'ry breeze.____ But you got to

86

stop and smell the ros - es.___ You got to count your man - y bless-ings ev - er - y

day.___ You're gon - na find the way to heav - en ___ is a

rough and rock - y road if you don't stop and smell the ros - es a - long___ the

1. 2.
way._____

3.
way.
Much slower

87

It Is No Secret
(What God Can Do)

Out of his own personal experience came "It Is No Secret," says Stuart Hamblen, the cowboy singer and songwriter who confesses that he was once in danger of becoming an alcoholic. A friend of his asked him how he broke the habit, and Hamblen replied: "I didn't do it. The Lord did it. He can do the same for anybody who'll let Him.

It's no secret what God can do." That night, waiting to go to bed, Hamblen heard the grandfather clock strike midnight, and at the same time the now-familiar refrain ran through his mind. He sat down at the piano. "In exactly 17 minutes it was finished, tune and all," he recalls about the writing of this popular country-gospel song.

Words and Music by Stuart Hamblen

C
C♯dim
G/D bass
D7
new. Do not be dis - heart - ened, for I have news for
side. Just take Him at His prom - ise. Don't run a - way and
G7
Cm6
Gdim
G7
CHORUS
F
G7
C
you:
hide. poco rall.
It is no se - cret what God can do.
a tempo
C♯dim
G7
C
What He's done for oth - ers, He'll do for you. With arms wide
F
F♯dim
C/G bass
C♯dim
G7
o - pen, He'll par - don you. It is no se - cret
Dm7
G7
1. C F C Dm7 C
2. A♭ Fm6 C
what God can do. There
do.
5fr.
4fr.

The King of All Kings

Born the son of a Methodist minister, Stuart Hamblen grew up in Texas with more of an urge to carouse than to worship. But in the 1950's, thanks to a crusade by evangelist Billy Graham, he experienced an overwhelming revival of faith and belief in God and turned with his wife, Suzy, to a career of religious songwriting and film pro-

ducing. In "The King of All Kings," one of his early successes, he draws on what he must have heard as a boy from his father's pulpit. He personalizes the message with a flexible but reverent tempo and an unforgettable turn of phrase — "The darkness can't hide me, He'll send me, I know, For men are His diamonds and He loves me so!"

Words and Music by Stuart Hamblen

When It's Round-up Time In Heaven

James Houston Davis was teaching history and social science at a State university in his native Louisiana when he heard some songs that radically changed his life. They were by the great country artist and composer Jimmie Rodgers. Davis informalized himself to "Jimmie" and began to turn out country-and-western classics in the Rodgers tradition. Among them are the secular "You Are My Sunshine" and the religiously oriented "When It's Round-up Time in Heaven," which has a hint or two of "Home on the Range" in it. Davis used his own music when he campaigned for the governorship of Louisiana (he served two terms), causing an unsuccessful rival to ask unhappily: "How can you election-eer against a song?"

Words and Music by Jimmie Davis

Moderate country waltz

mf

When it's round - up time in Heav - en and our trou - bles on earth are o'er, All the friends that death has sev - ered

93

Daddy Sang Bass

Carl Perkins' appealing picture of a family united in song ("You could hear us singin' for a country mile") not only provided a tremendous hit song for a fellow Nashville singer, Johnny Cash, but it also painted a touching memory of hard times when poor people tried to coax crops out of the "black land dirt." The song, a combination of rock and gospel, was written in 1968, and Cash's rugged baritone brought it to prominence that year. But the times it tells of could have been much earlier in our history, or they could be now, while the thought of the family reunited, still singing together "at the throne" beyond, is a dream that everyone cherishes for the future.

Words and Music by Carl Perkins

Moderately

VERSE

I re- / mem - ber when I was a lad, times were hard and things were
mem - ber af - ter work, mama would call in all of

bad; But there's a sil - ver lin - ing be - hind ev - 'ry cloud.
us; You could hear us sing - in' for a coun - try mile.

Just poor peo - ple, that's all we were, try'n' to make a
Now little broth - er has done gone on, but I'll re-

livin' out of black land dirt;   We'd get to-geth-er in a fam-'ly
join him in a song;   We'll be to-geth-er a-gain up

cir-cle, sing-in' loud. _____   Dad-dy sang bass, ma-ma sang
yon-der in a lit-tle while. _____

CHORUS

ten-or, me and lit-tle broth-er would join right in there;   Sing-in' seems to

help a trou-bled soul. _____   One of these days and it won't be

long, I'll re-join them in a song;   I'm gon-na join the fam-'ly

These Hands

Like the beloved "Praying Hands" engraving by German artist Albrecht Dürer (1471–1528), which has come to symbolize the beauty of manual work, Eddie Noack's song "These Hands" celebrates the evidence of labor and care on the gnarled old hands the singer raises "to praise the Lord." Among the many artists who brought the song to popularity at the height of the country-gospel enthusiasm in the mid-sixties, perhaps the most prominent was Canadian-born Hank Snow, the "Singing Ranger." Snow settled into the special beauty of Nashville song as comfortably as if he had created it all by himself.

**Words and Music
by Eddie Noack**

These hands ain't the hands of a gen-tle-man; These hands are cal-loused and old. These hands raised a fam-'ly;____ These hands raised a home. Now these hands raise to praise the Lord.____ These hands won the

heart of my loved one; And with hers they were nev-er a-lone._____ If these hands filled their task,___ then what more could one ask, For these fin-gers_____ have worked to the bone._____ Now don't try to judge me_____ by what you'd like to be, For my life ain't been much suc-cess._____ While some

peo-ple— have pow-er, but still they— grieve, while these
hands brought me hap-pi-ness._____ *Slower* Now I'm
tired and I'm old and I ain't got much gold; May-be things ain't been
In tempo
all that I planned.___ God a-bove, hear my plea, when it's
time to judge me, Take a look at these hard-work-in' hands.___

A Satisfied Mind

Words and Music by Red Hays and Jack Rhodes

Several singers are identified with Red Hays and Jack Rhodes' 1955 triple-meter song about what money can and can't buy. Among them is Red Foley, who brought so many sacred songs to the popularity charts in the 1950's ("Peace in the Valley," "Steal Away," and "Just a Closer Walk With Thee" are three others). At about the same time, a lanky blond young country singer launched his career with this song. Porter Wagoner was his name, and he has become one of country music's brightest and most totally committed artists. In the 20 years since then, he has had dozens of Top Ten discs, and his own television show has been carried by more than a hundred stations across the nation.

(1) How man-y times have you heard some-one
(2) Once I was win - ning in for-tune and

say, Ev'ry - thing that I dreamed for
fame; If I had his mon - ey,

I would do things my way;
to get a start in life's game.
But
But

(3) Money can't buy back your youth when you're old,
    Or a friend when you're lonely, Or a love that's grown cold;
    The wealthiest person Is a pauper at times,
    Compared to the man With a satisfied mind.

(4) When life has ended, my time has run out,
    My friends and my loved ones I'll leave, there's no doubt;
    But one thing for certain, When it comes my time,
    I'll leave this old world With a satisfied mind.

Mansion Over the Hilltop

Once upon a time there was a rich man whose business was failing. To escape the suffocating pressure he was under, he drove out into the countryside one afternoon. Getting out of his car and walking, he noticed that the farmhouses he passed were in pathetic disrepair. In front of the most dilapidated of all he discovered a tiny girl playing cheerfully with her ragged wisp of a doll. "How can you be so happy?" the man asked, "your dolly is coming to pieces, and your house is falling down."

"Oh, that's all right," she said, looking at him with her clear gaze and then pointing behind her. "My daddy just got a lot of money, and he's building me a big mansion right over that hill." The man began to think of his own Father who had a mansion prepared for him just beyond the clouds. Suddenly nothing else seemed very important. "Why worry?" he asked himself. That story, told by a fellow Texas minister, prompted the Reverend Ira Stanphill to write this hymn.

Words and Music by Ira Stanphill

(1) I want a gold one that's sil - ver lined.
(2) I know He'll give me a man - sion my own.
(3) I want a man - sion, a harp, and a crown.

CHORUS

mf I've got a man - sion just o - ver the hill - top,

In that bright land where we'll nev - er grow old;

And some - day yon - der we will nev - er - more wan - der

But walk on streets that are pur - est gold.

Last time, slower

103

These Things Shall Pass

When Stuart Hamblen writes in "These Things Shall Pass" that "we'll look back and smile at the heartaches we have known," he could be recalling some moments of his own youth. There were times, he relates, when he was on the verge of becoming an alcoholic, but his reconversion to faith and trust in the God of Love made it possible for him not only to conquer his problem but also to run for the Presidency of the United States on the Prohibition ticket in 1952. In addition, his return to religion brought forth such songs as "The King of All Kings," "It Is No Secret," and this one, all of which were heard in the film Country Church, which he produced with his wife.

Words and Music by Stuart Hamblen

Moderately, with expression

These things shall pass,___ And some great morn - in'___ ___ We'll look back and smile at heart - aches we have known; So don't for - get,___ When shad - ows gath - er,___

The Lord our God is still the King up-on His throne.

A rose looks gray at mid-night, but the flame is just a-

p gradually getting louder - - - - -

sleep, And steel is strong, be-cause it knew the ham-mer and white

heat. These things shall pass and life be sweet-er,

When love and faith are strong, they can-not long en-dure.

105

I Found the Answer

Words and Music by Johnny Lange

Johnny Lange, one of today's leading devotional composers, remembers particularly well the source of his "I Found the Answer." A young man, recently released from prison, stopped by to visit him one day and to say that while he was an inmate a visiting entertainer's performance of Lange's "I Asked the Lord" had moved him so much that he had learned to pray, to read the Bible daily, and to play the guitar so that he too could sing songs like that one. "You have found the answer," Lange said, after the young man told him of his reconciliation with his wife and family and of his general rehabilitation. Smiling, the former convict said: "Yes, I'm happy . . . I found the answer, and I'm going to try to help others find the answer." That remark stayed with Lange, and a few months later when George Beverly Shea, Billy Graham's featured singer, asked him to write a song, those were the words that gave him inspiration. "Suddenly I found the answer too," Lange says. Shea recorded the song in 1957, and there were other notable performances, more than 50, including those by Mahalia Jackson and Nat "King" Cole.

Slowly, with feeling

(1) I was weak and wea - ry, I had gone a - stray, Walk - ing in the dark - ness, I
(2) I was sad and lone - ly, All my hopes were gone, Days were long and drear - y, I
(3) Keep your Bi - ble with you, Read it ev - 'ry day, Al - ways count your bless - ings and

(1) could - n't find my way. Then a light came shin - ing, to lead me from de - spair,
(2) could - n't car - ry on. Then I found the cour - age to keep my head up high,
(3) al - ways stop to pray. Learn to keep be - liev - ing and faith will see you through,

CHORUS

(1) All my sins for-giv-en, and I was free from care. I found the an-swer,__ I learned to
(2) Once a-gain I'm hap-py and here's the rea-son why. I found the an-swer,__ I learned to
(3) Seek to know con-tent-ment and it will come to you. I found the an-swer,__ I learned to

(1) pray. With faith to guide me_____ I found the way. The sun is
(2) pray. With faith to guide me_____ I found the way. The sun is
(3) pray. With God be-side me_____ I found the way. The sun is

(1) shin-ing for me each day,_____ I found the an-swer,__ I learned to
(2) shin-ing for me each day,_____ I found the an-swer,__ I learned to
(3) shin-ing for me each day,_____ I found the

1. 2.

(1) pray.
(2) pray.

3.

(3) an-swer,__ I learned to pray.

slower

THAT OLD-TIME RELIGION

108

This old favorite seems to have sprung from Southern soil. The reference to "old-time" suggests that it could have originated in the late 19th century when some Negro spirituals found acceptance in white revival circles. There have been innu- *merable variations in the lyrics, and many names have been put after the words "it was good for"—including Paul and Silas, Old Abe Lincoln, and Harry Truman. The choice depended on the place, the time, and the song leader's imagination.*

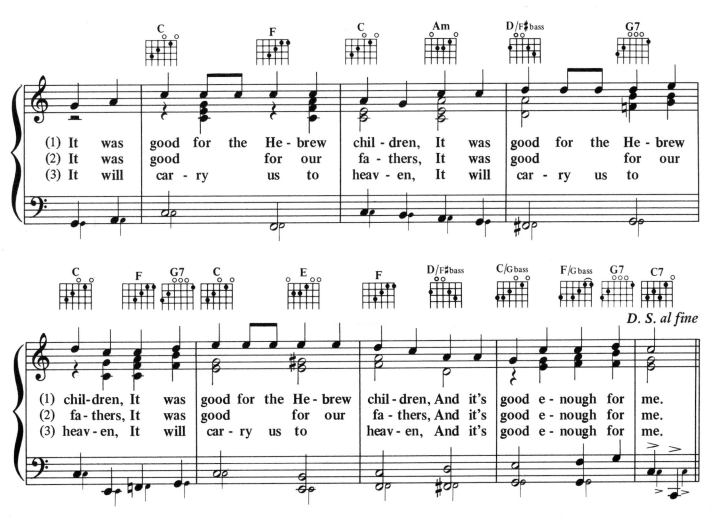

(1) It was good for the He - brew chil - dren, It was good for the He - brew
(2) It was good for our fa - thers, It was good for our
(3) It will car - ry us to heav - en, It will car - ry us to

D. S. al fine

(1) chil - dren, It was good for the He - brew chil - dren, And it's good e - nough for me.
(2) fa - thers, It was good for our fa - thers, And it's good e - nough for me.
(3) heav - en, It will car - ry us to heav - en, And it's good e - nough for me.

The Old Rugged Cross

Words and Music by George Bennard

"I was praying for a full understanding of the cross and its plan in Christianity," explains the Rev. George Bennard of his famous gospel hymn, written in 1913 and widely publicized by Homer Rodeheaver, the popular evangelist, singer, and trombonist. Suddenly the theme for a song, and the melody as well, came to him. But the words did not come. He could get no further than the phrase "old rugged cross," and somewhere within him a voice bade him wait to finish the song. Finally some months later, after a series of exhausting but triumphant revival meetings, his poetic inspiration merged with his recent and exhilarating successes, and "The Old Rugged Cross" was the result.

(3) In the old rugged cross, stained with blood so divine,
A wondrous beauty I see.
For 'twas on that old cross Jesus suffered and died
To pardon and sanctify me.
Chorus

(4) To the old rugged cross, I will ever be true,
Its shame and reproach gladly bear,
Then He'll call me some day to my home far away,
Where His glory forever I'll share.
Chorus

ROCK OF AGES

"Rock of Ages"—the strength of the poetic image and the compassion of its musical setting have made this a favorite of all ages for nearly 150 years. Augustus Montague Toplady's poem (in a shorter version) was first published in Gospel Magazine in 1776. Just a few months later he worked it into an article in connection with, of all things, the British national debt — to show that, like monetary obligations, our sins, unchecked, can multiply astronomically. Toplady called his verse "A Living and Dying Prayer for the Holiest Believer in the World." Perhaps it was this somewhat puzzling title that brought the poem to the attention of an American hymnist, Thomas Hastings, who made the musical setting so much admired today. He published it in a devotional songbook, Spiritual Songs for Social Worship, in 1833. In the years since, "Rock of Ages" has confirmed the judgment expressed by one of its early admirers, who declared: "Take from me all other music if needs be, but leave me only this for strength."

Words by Augustus Montague Toplady
Music by Thomas Hastings

Rock of A - ges, cleft for me! Let me hide my - self in Thee; Let the wa - ter and the blood, From Thy wound - ed side which

flowed, Be of sin the dou-ble cure, Save from wrath, and make me

pure. Could my tears for-ev-er flow, Could my

zeal no lan-guor know, These for sin could not a-tone, Thou must

save and Thou a-lone; In my hand no price I bring, Simp-ly

to Thy cross I cling.

O WORSHIP THE KING

(1) O wor - ship the King, all glo - rious a - bove, O

(2) (O) tell of His might, O sing of His grace, Whose

grate - ful - ly sing His pow'r___ and His love. Our

robe is the light, whose can - o - py, space. His

George Frederick Handel, mighty composer of The Messiah *and other Baroque masterpieces, for many years received credit for also having written "Joy to the World," now known to have been composed by an American, Lowell Mason, and "O Worship the King," another joyous and solidly paced tune somewhat like it. In recent years scholarship has found the true composer, a fine musician named William Croft, whose reputation diminishes only in comparison to the giant* Handel. His services to English church music were extraordinary, and he wrote the tune "Hanover," to which "O Worship the King" is sung, at least 2 years before Handel ever left his native Germany to set foot on English soil. Paraphrases of the Psalms have always been popular with religious poets; and the words to this song are a "new" version — written by Robert Grant in 1833 — of such a paraphrase by William Kethe, a Scottish minister of the last half of the 16th century.

Words by Robert Grant **Music by William Croft**

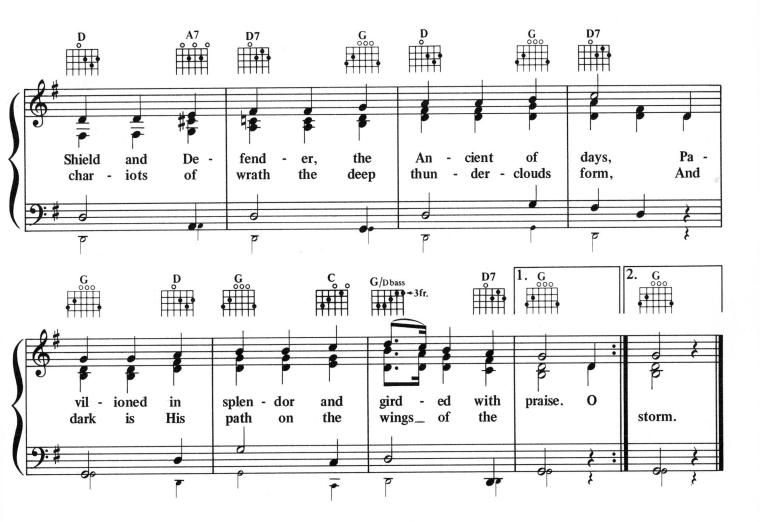

(3) Thy bountiful care what tongue can recite?
It breathes in the air, it shines in the light.
It streams from the hills, it descends to the plain,
And sweetly distills in the dew and the rain.

(4) Frail children of dust and feeble as frail,
In Thee do we trust, nor find Thee to fail.
Thy mercies how tender, how firm to the end,
Our Maker, Defender, Redeemer, and Friend.

Blessed Assurance

Words by Fanny Crosby van Alstyne   **Music by Mrs. Joseph F. Knapp**

In a slow 3 (♩. = one beat)

(1) Bless - ed as - sur - ance Je - sus is mine, Oh, what a
(2) Per - fect sub - mis - sion, per - fect de - light, Vi - sions of
(3) Per - fect sub - mis - sion all is at rest, I in my

(1) fore - taste of glo - ry di - vine. Heir of sal - va - tion, pur - chase of
(2) rap - ture now burst on my sight. An - gels de - scend - ing bring from a -
(3) Sav - ior am hap - py and blest. Watch - ing and wait - ing look - ing a -

(1) God, Born of His spir - it, washed in His blood.
(2) bove Ech - oes of mer - cy, whis - pers of love.
(3) bove, Filled with His good - ness, lost in His love.

"*I have often composed as many as six or seven hymns in one day,*" *wrote Fanny Crosby van Alstyne at the end of a long life (she died in 1915 at the age of 95). One of her contemporaries called her* "*the greatest living writer of hymns,*" *and went on to say:* "*All over this country, and, one might say, the world, Fanny Crosby's hymns are singing themselves into the hearts and souls of the people.*" *Fanny Crosby was blind from infancy; nonetheless, she began to write poetry when she was only 8 years old and continued to do so for another 80*

years. Her facility was so extraordinary that she could guarantee a publishing house three hymns a week. She once obliged her friend W. H. Doane, a composer of gospel tunes, by dashing off "*Safe in the Arms of Jesus*" *to one of his melodies in about 15 minutes while he waited to board a train. Her musical partner for* "*Blessed Assurance*" *was another productive and pious lady, Mrs. Joseph F. Knapp, who helped her husband, founder of the Metropolitan Life Insurance Company, superintend two large Sunday schools in Brooklyn, New York.*

Jesus, Lover of My Soul

Words by Charles Wesley
Music by Simeon Buckley Marsh

(1) Je - sus, lov - er
(2) Oth - er ref - uge
(3) Plen - teous grace with

(1) of my soul,
(2) have I none,
(3) Thee is found,

Let me to Thy bos - om fly,_____
Hangs my help - less soul on Thee;_____
Grace to cleanse from all my sin;_____

(1) While the near - er wa - ters roll,
(2) Leave, ah, leave me not a - lone,
(3) Let the heal - ing streams a - bound,

While the tem - pest still is
Still sup - port and com - fort
Make and keep me pure with -

The famous Wesley brothers, John and Charles, founded the Methodist religious movement in England and then endowed it with literally thousands of superb hymns. Charles, the more prolific, wrote some 6,500. Oddly enough, for many years strict churchmen found the sentiments in Charles' "Jesus, Lover of My Soul" too personal, too intimate for a congregational hymn, and it is only since about 1825 (the hymn was first published in 1756) that its quiet intensity and sober appeal have found a really wide audience. The tune that we use here, one of several well-known ones, was written by a devout teacher of singing, Simeon Buckley Marsh, who organized singing schools near Albany, New York, in the mid-1800's. He was in fact on horseback, traveling between two of these schools, when the melody came into his mind.

On page 120 you will find a light, rock-style version of this hymn, in which arranger Dan Fox shows how appropriately Marsh's modest melody (it uses only six notes), fitted out with today's rhythms and a flatted chord or two, can give new power to the already powerful hymn.

(1) high; Hide me, O my Sav - ior, hide,
(2) me; All my trust on Thee is stayed,
(3) in; Thou of life the foun - tain art,

(1) Till the storm of life is past; Safe in - to the
(2) All my help from Thee I bring, Cov - er my de -
(3) Free - ly let me take of Thee; Spring Thou up with -

(1) ha - ven guide, O re - ceive my soul at last.
(2) fense - less head With the shad - ow of Thy wing.
(3) in my heart, Rise to all e - ter - ni - ty.

Jesus, Lover of My Soul

Contemporary Version

Words by Charles Wesley
Music by Simeon Buckley Marsh

*Guitarists tune 6th string down to D.

(2) Other refuge have I none,   All my trust on Thee is stayed,
Hangs my helpless soul on Thee;   All my help from Thee I bring,
Leave, ah, leave me not alone,   Cover my defenseless head,
Still support and comfort me;   With the shadow of Thy wing.

(3) Plenteous grace with Thee is found,
Grace to cleanse from all my sin;
Let the healing streams abound,
Make and keep me pure within.

Thou of life the fountain art;
Freely let me take of Thee;
Spring Thou up within my heart,
Rise to all eternity.

Lead, Kindly Light

Becalmed between Corsica and Sardinia on an orange boat in June of 1833, John Henry Newman, the famous English scholar and cleric, wrote the lyric "Lead, Kindly Light." Its stately though unusual meter and its compelling imagery made it the finest of a collection he published in 1834. Newman was a vigorous defender of his religious beliefs, and his conversion to the Roman Catholic Church from the Church of England was an event of considerable importance in Victorian En-

Rather slowly (but don't drag)

(1) Lead, kind - ly light a - mid th'en - cir - cling gloom, Lead Thou me on. The night is dark, and I am far from

(2) (I was not) ev - er thus nor prayed that Thou Shouldst lead me on. I loved to choose and see my path, but

(3) (So long Thy) pow'r hath blest me, sure it still Will lead me on. O'er moor and fen, o'er crag and tor - rent

Words by John Henry Newman   Music by John B. Dykes

gland. Since he considered his verse "humble," Newman was surprised at the wide acceptance of his "Lead, Kindly Light." He attributed its success to the musical setting composed especially for it by John B. Dykes. That melody, it is said, came to Dykes as he was walking through a crowded street in London; he published it in 1867. Many other excellent musical settings, however, have only served to emphasize repeatedly the lofty character and conviction of Newman's poem.

Holy God, We Praise Thy Name

Words based on a translation by Clarence Walworth

(1) Ho - ly God,___ we praise___ Thy name, Lord of
(2) Hark the loud___ ce - les - tial hymn An - gel

all,___ we bow___ be - fore Thee. All on earth___ Thy
choirs___ a - bove___ are rais - ing, Cher - u - bim___ and

To the Austrian Empress Maria Theresa belonged the songbook in which this sturdy hymn first appeared. That was in 1774, and the words of course were German, while the tune, already ancient, was partly folksong and partly religious chant. Four years later a slightly different version was published, and it became so popular that it was translated into many languages. The first example published in English came from the pen of an American, Clarence Augustus Walworth, who was trained as a lawyer in a small upstate New York town and then decided to devote his life to religion, becoming a mission preacher of remarkable eloquence. Although he was blind for the last 10 years of his life, he continued to "praise Thy name" for the religious conversion that had afforded him such joy. The text here is based on Walworth's, and the tune is only slightly modified from the original.

(3) Lo, the apostolic train
    Joins Thy sacred name to hallow.
    Prophets swell the glad refrain,
    And the white-robed martyrs follow.
    And from morn to set of sun
    Thru the church the song goes on.

(4) Holy Father, Holy Son,
    Holy Spirit, Three we name Thee.
    While in essence only one,
    Undivided God we claim Thee.
    And adoring bend the knee,
    While we sing our praise to Thee.

HOLY, HOLY, HOLY

Words by Reginald Heber   Music by John B. Dykes

(1) Ho - ly, ho - ly, ho - ly! Lord God al - might - y!
(2) Ho - ly, ho - ly, ho - ly! All the Saints a - dore Thee,
(3) Ho - ly, ho - ly, ho - ly! Lord God al - might - y!

(1) Ear - ly in the morn - ing our song shall rise to
(2) Cast - ing down their gold - en crowns a - round the glass - y
(3) All Thy works shall praise Thy name, in earth and sky and

Reginald Heber, an English divine of great energy and charm, published "Holy, Holy, Holy," one of the most famous of his many famous hymns, in 1826. In that same year he died of apoplexy in India—where he had been Bishop of Calcutta—at the height of his creative powers, and at the age of 43. Splendidly educated and blessed with a fine literary taste, Bishop Heber could compose at the drop of a hat. His father-in-law, also a cleric, approached him one Saturday evening with the request that he "write something for us to sing at the service tomorrow." In a few moments Heber had completed the words to "From Greenland's Icy Mountain," which, next to "Holy, Holy, Holy," is probably his most famous poem. John Bacchus Dykes, exemplary churchman and composer, wrote a tune especially for "Holy, Holy, Holy" and named it "Nicaea," after the church council of A.D. 325 at which the three aspects of the Holy Trinity were clearly defined. Strong, sturdy, always fresh, the hymn is one of the glories of Victorian church music and of ageless religious conviction.

Nearer, My God, to Thee

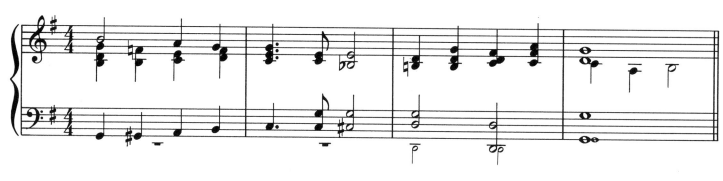

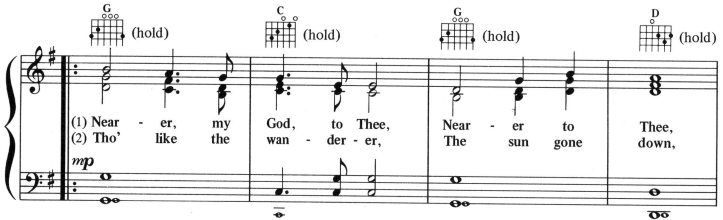

(1) Near - er, my God, to Thee, Near - er to Thee,
(2) Tho' like the wan - der - er, The sun gone down,

mp

E'en tho' it be a cross That raiseth me,
Dark - ness be o - ver me, My rest a stone,

Play left hand softly, almost like a heartthrob

Words by Sarah Fuller Adams   Music by Lowell Mason

Privately a rather radical believer in wider rights for women, Sarah Fuller Adams, an Englishwoman, confined her public activities for the most part to writing hymns and anthems on religious subjects. These she contributed to the publications of her friend and Unitarian pastor, William Johnson Fox, a more outspoken partisan for women's rights and increased freedom of the press as well. "Nearer, My God, to Thee," written in 1840, is a poem based on the dream of Jacob at Bethel, as related in the Book of Genesis. The tune given here came about not on a dream-filled night but on a sleepless one, at least for Lowell Mason, the American hymnwriter. "One night, sometime after lying awake in the dark, eyes wide open, through the stillness in the house the melody came to me, and the next morning I wrote down the notes," he recalled later. That was in 1859, and the hymn became popular in this country to his tune, not to an earlier one by John Dykes. (It was the Dykes version that the ship's band played, according to survivors, on that tragic night when the Titanic collided with an iceberg and sank.)

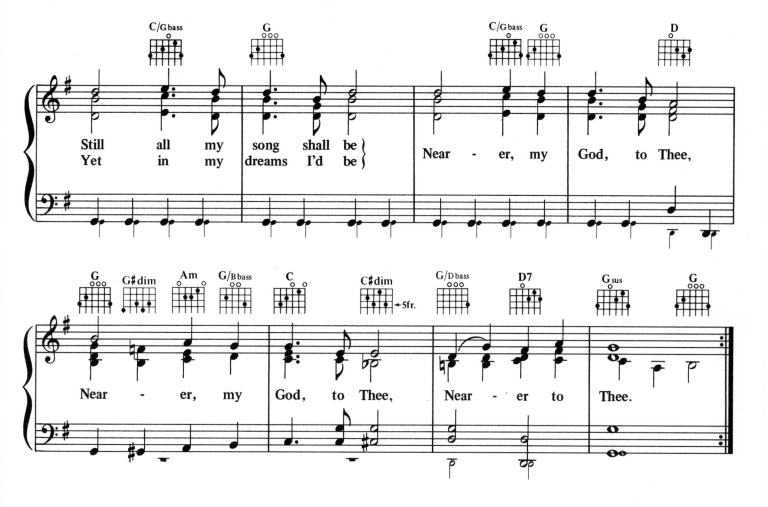

(3) There let the way appear,
Steps unto Heav'n,
All that Thou sendest me,
In mercy giv'n,
Angels to beckon me
Nearer, my God, to Thee, *etc.*

(4) Then with my waking thoughts,
Bright with Thy praise,
Out of my stony griefs,
Bethel I'll raise,
So by my woes to be
Nearer, my God, to Thee, *etc.*

Bringing In the Sheaves

(1) Sow - ing in the morn - ing,
(2) Sow - ing in the sun - shine,
(3) Go - ing forth with weep - ing,

(1) sow - ing seeds of kind - ness,
(2) sow - ing in the shad - ows,
(3) sow - ing for the Mas - ter,

Sow - ing in the noon - tide
Fear - ing nei - ther clouds nor
Tho' the loss sus - tained our

and the dew - y eve,
win - ter's chill - ing breeze,
spir - it of - ten grieves,

(1) Wait - ing for the har - vest
(2) By and by the har - vest
(3) When our weep - ing's o - ver

and the time of reap - ing,
and the la - bor end - ed.
He will bid us wel - come.

We shall come re - joic - ing,
We shall come re - joic - ing,
We shall come re - joic - ing,

Knowles Shaw based "Bringing In the Sheaves" on a portion of Psalm 126: "They that sow in tears shall reap in joy. He that now goeth forth and weepeth, bearing precious seed, shall doubtless come again with rejoicing, bringing his sheaves with him." It was the message of many evangelical preachers that if we accomplished good deeds in adversity, we would enjoy their harvest in good times; that if we persisted in life here on a difficult earth, our reward would come in heaven. When set to a rousing gospel tune, "Bringing In the Sheaves" became one of the most popular revival meeting songs, and no one who has heard it thundered out by hundreds of fervent believers under an open-air tent on a summer night can ever forget the experience.

Words by Knowles Shaw
Music by George A. Minor

131

Come Unto Me, Ye Weary

Come un - to me, ye wea - ry, And I will give you
Come un - to me, dear chil - dren, And I will give you

rest. O bless - ed voice of Je - sus, which
light. O lov - ing voice of Je - sus, which

comes to hearts op - pressed. It tells of ben - e -
comes to cheer the night. Our hearts were filled with

Catherine H. Watterman wrote the stanzas of "Come Unto Me, Ye Weary," the hymn by which she is today remembered, in 1839, the year before she was married to a Philadelphia businessman. Her inspiration was the beautiful message in Matthew II: 28 / 30: "Come to Me, all you who labor . . . For My yoke is easy, and My burden is light." Her poem appeared in The Christian Keepsake, *where it came to the attention of Lowell Mason, the Congregational layman whose reputation as America's finest 19th-century hymnwriter is based on tunes such as this one.*

Words by Catherine H. Watterman
Music by Lowell Mason

dic - tion, Of par - don, grace, and peace, Of
sad - ness, And we had lost our way, But

joy that hath no end - ing, Of love, which can - not cease.
He hath brought us glad - ness And songs at break of day.

Flee as a Bird

"Flee as a Bird" was originally published by the staid Boston firm of Oliver Ditson in 1857. Mary S. B. Dana's tune had been arranged for her by her friend, the great religious musician George F. Root, an incredibly active composer of hymns and anthems and whole books of advice for churches. (His old age was made especially happy by two daughters who sang hymns for him by the hour.) The charming little melody quickly swept the country and became so well known, so utterly familiar, that we find New Orleans jazz artist Jelly Roll Morton, for example, using it (unattributed to Mrs. Dana or anyone else) in the introduction for his superb 1926 recording "Dead Man Blues." (It was a staple at New Orleans funerals, alternating with "Just a Closer Walk with Thee.") And in recent years "Flee as a Bird" has come into a third life, this time as a country music classic, its plaintive charm and easy attractiveness undiminished by time or use or change in style.

Words and Music by Mary S. B. Dana; Arranged by George F. Root

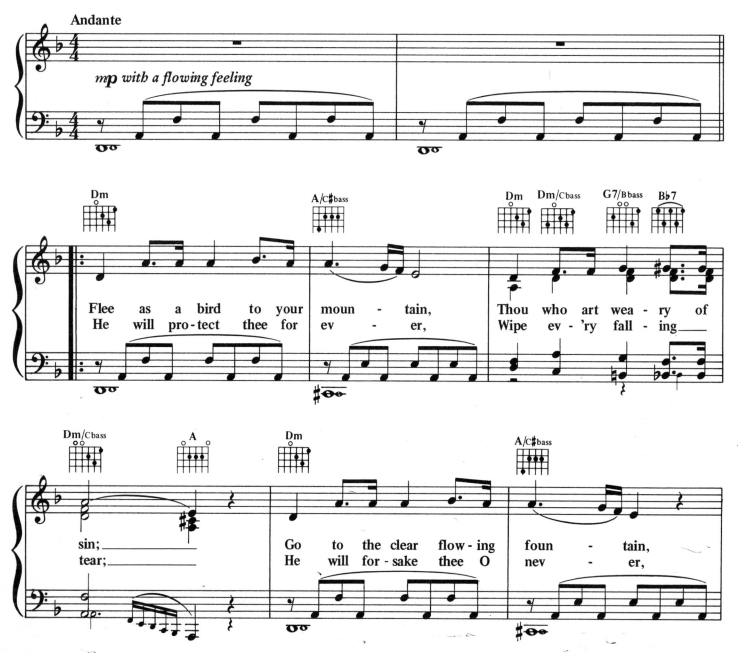

Almighty Father, Strong To Save

A modest English schoolmaster, born in 1825, contributed "Almighty" [or "Eternal"] "Father, Strong To Save," to a hymnal in 1860, giving it this caption: "For those at Sea. 'These men see the works of the Lord, and his wonders in the deep.'" Now familiarly known as the "Navy Hymn," William Whiting's poem invokes the protective hand of God "for those in peril on the sea." In 1937 Robert Nelson Spencer, recognizing that faith can protect us everywhere, brought the hymn up to date by adding stanzas that cover modern transportation by land and by air as well. The tune for all stanzas is another by John Bacchus Dykes.

Words by William Whiting   Music by John B. Dykes

(1) Almighty Father, strong to save, Whose arm hath bound the restless wave, Who bidd'st the mighty ocean deep, Its

(2) O Christ, the Lord of hill and plain, O'er which our traffic runs amain, By mountain pass or valley low, Where-

Words by Robert Nelson Spencer

(3) O Spirit, whom the Father sent
    To spread abroad the firmament;
    O Wind of Heaven, by thy might,
    Save all who dare the eagle's flight;
      And keep them by Thy watchful care
      From every peril in the air.

(4) O Trinity of love and power,
    Our brethren shield in danger's hour;
    From rock and tempest, fire and foe,
    Protect them whereso'er they go;
      Thus evermore shall rise to thee
      Glad praise from air and land and sea.

HOLD THE FORT

Words and Music by Philip P. Bliss

Very steady, like a march

pp gradually getting louder, | *like an approaching parade*

1st time p and continue crescendo; 2nd time mf

(1) Ho, my com - rades, see the sig - nal, Wav - ing in the sky,
(2) See the might - y host ad - vanc - ing, Sa - tan lead - ing on,

Re - in - force - ments now ap - pear - ing, Vic - to - ry is nigh.
Might - y men a - round us fall - ing, Cour - age al - most gone.

During the Civil War Gen. William T. Sherman's army lay near Atlanta in October 1864, waiting to begin what would become the famous "march to the sea," when the news arrived that a vast store of necessary supplies and food — a million rations — was in danger of being destroyed by advancing Confederate troops. Only a few Union soldiers, only a small fort, protected the provisions piled up at Allatoona Pass. But, as the story is told, one of those besieged heroes, looking through a telescope for promised reinforcements, saw instead a message in signal flags, waving from a mountain opposite: "Hold the fort, for I am coming."

Hold the fort they did, and the story of their triumph was told at a Sunday school convention in 1870. Philip P. Bliss, song leader for the convention and already the composer of several famous Civil War ballads, was so inspired that he dashed off "Hold the Fort" the next day. His friend Ira D. Sankey, the famous evangelist-musician, frequently conducted the song in later years, using a baton made of wood that came from the very tree atop Kennesaw Mountain from which the signaler had sent Sherman's message. Bliss wrote many lovely gospel songs, but it is as the composer of "Hold the Fort" that his tombstone identifies him for all time.

CHORUS

Hold the fort, for I am com-ing, Je-sus sig-nals still;

Wave the an-swer back to Heav-en, By Thy grace we will.

(3) See the glorious banner waving! Hear the trumpet blow!
In our Leader's name we'll triumph Over ev'ry foe.
Chorus

(4) Fierce and long the battle rages, But our help is near;
Onward comes our great Commander, Cheer, my comrades, cheer.
Chorus

My Faith Looks Up to Thee

Poet, essayist, and descendant of John and Priscilla Alden, Ray Palmer was only 22 and a recent graduate of Yale University when he wrote his first hymn, "My Faith Looks Up to Thee," in 1830. Fortunately, he was able to bring it to the attention of Lowell Mason, master hymnist and collector. Dr. Mason made a musical setting forthwith and included it in his Spiritual Songs for Social Worship of 1833, naming the setting "Olivet" after the Mount of Olives, where Jesus prayed the night before He was to be crucified. Not only did Mason contribute hugely to sacred music for all of his long life (1792–1872), but he became known as the "father of singing among the children" because of his collections of songs and the large singing classes he organized for children in the Boston area.

Words by Ray Palmer   **Music by Lowell Mason**

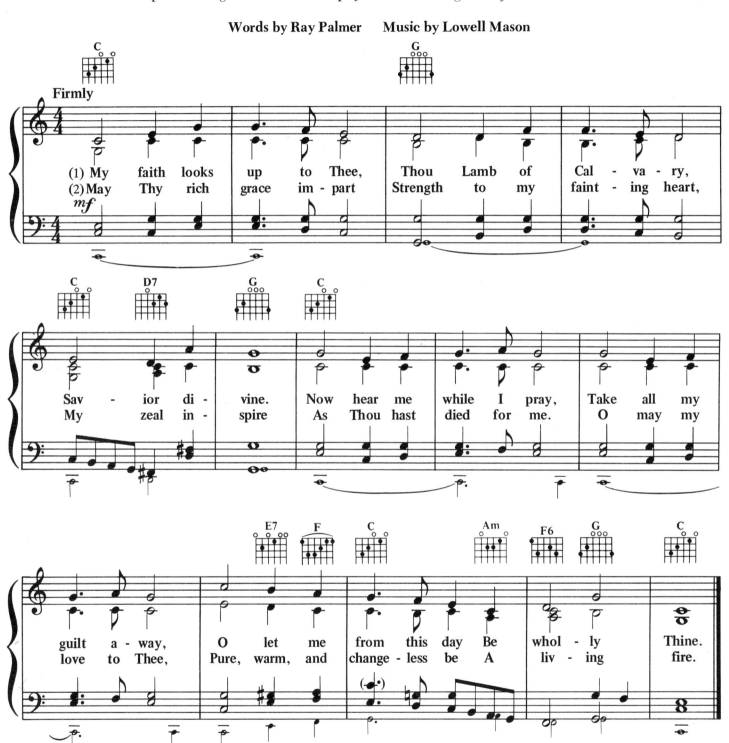

(1) My faith looks up to Thee, Thou Lamb of Cal - va - ry,
(2) May Thy rich grace im - part Strength to my faint - ing heart,

Sav - ior di - vine. Now hear me while I pray, Take all my
My zeal in - spire As Thou hast died for me. O may my

guilt a - way, O let me from this day Be whol - ly Thine.
love to Thee, Pure, warm, and change - less be A liv - ing fire.

(3) While life's dark maze I tread
And griefs around me spread,
Be Thou my guide.
Bid darkness turn to day,
Wipe sorrow's tears away,
Nor let me ever stray
From Thee aside.

(4) When ends life's transient dream,
When death's cold sullen stream
Shall o'er me roll,
Blest Savior then in love,
Fear and distrust remove,
O bear me safe above
A ransomed soul.

Blest Be the Tie That Binds

Words by John Fawcett
Music by Hans Georg Nägeli, Arranged by Lowell Mason

John Fawcett, an impoverished preacher in a tiny village in England, never made more than about a hundred dollars a year, but his family grew and grew. Finally, about 1772, he received the offer of a much larger church, in London. The income was a good deal handsomer than in his Yorkshire parish, and he accepted the call. His goods packed, his affairs in order, he made the mistake of preaching a most sentiment-laden sermon on his final Sunday, and the tears and sighs of his parishioners so undid him that he unpacked everything and remained in Wainsgate. He commemorated the occasion with a poem, "Blest Be the Tie That Binds," which has become one of the most striking and frequently sung of all "Fellowship" hymns. Lowell Mason's arrangement of a Hans Georg Nägeli tune, "Dennis," provided the music so familiar today.

(1) Blest be the tie that binds Our hearts in Christian love. The fellowship of kindred minds Is like to that above.

(2) Before our Father's throne We pour our ardent prayers. Our fears, our hopes, our aims are one, Our comforts and our cares.

(3) We share our mutual woes,
Our mutual burdens bear,
And often for each other flows
The sympathizing tear.

(4) When we asunder part
It gives us inward pain.
But we shall still be joined in heart
And hope to meet again.

Love Divine, All Loves Excelling

This well-known piece by the prolific hymnwriter Charles Wesley, "Love Divine, All Loves Excelling" was first printed in a 1756 pamphlet called "Hymns for Those That Seek." The tune, often called "Love Divine," is also referred to as "Beecher," after the famous minister Henry Ward Beecher (brother of Uncle Tom's Cabin author Harriet Beecher Stowe) who headed a church in Brooklyn, New York. John Zundel, organist of the parish, composed the music and named it for Dr. Beecher, knowing his pastor's intense admiration for Wesley verses in general. About "Jesus, Lover of My Soul," for instance, Beecher once exclaimed: "I would rather have written that hymn of Wesley's than to have the fame of all the kings that ever sat on the earth!"

Words by Charles Wesley   Music by John Zundel

(1) Love divine, all loves ex-cel-ling, Joy of Heav'n to Earth come down;
(2) Breathe, O breathe Thy lov-ing Spir-it In-to ev-'ry trou-bled breast!

Fix in us Thy hum-ble dwell-ing, All Thy faith-ful
Let us all in Thee in-her-it, Let us find that

(3) Come, Almighty, to deliver,
Let us all Thy life receive;
Suddenly return and never,
Nevermore Thy temples leave;
Thee we would be always blessing,
Serve Thee as Thy hosts above,
Pray and praise Thee without ceasing,
Glory in Thy perfect love!

(4) Finish then Thy new creation,
Pure and spotless may we be;
Let us see our whole salvation,
Perfectly secured in Thee;
Changed from glory into glory,
Till in heav'n we take our place,
Till we cast our crowns before Thee,
Lost in wonder, love, and praise!

When the Roll Is Called Up Yonder

Words and Music by James M. Black

One day in the 1890's when James M. Black, a Sunday school teacher in Williamsport, Pennsylvania, was taking a shortcut through a little-used alley, he encountered a shy, raggedly dressed girl sweeping the porch of a dreary hovel. He invited her to come to the class. Something about her stooped posture and her face, earnest but sad, haunted him, and the next Sunday as he called the roll of his class he included her name on the list. Alas, she was not there, and again the vision of her pinched face and overburdened demeanor came before his eyes. Something in the experience moved him, and he went home and immediately wrote a song—"I dared not change a note or a word," he said. Black wrote many hymns while a song-leader for churches and revival meetings, but this one has always remained his monument.

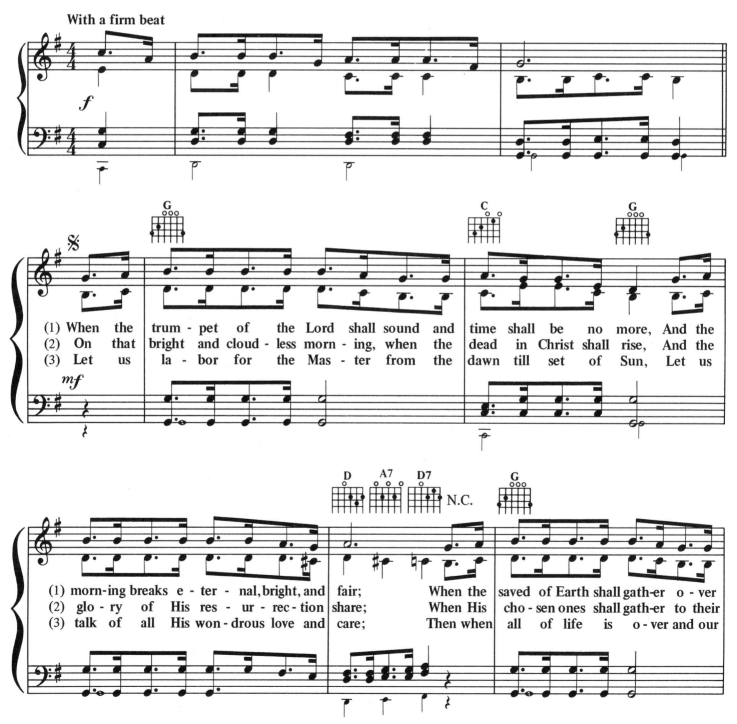

(1) When the trum-pet of the Lord shall sound and time shall be no more, And the
(2) On that bright and cloud-less morn-ing, when the dead in Christ shall rise, And the
(3) Let us la-bor for the Mas-ter from the dawn till set of Sun, Let us

(1) morn-ing breaks e-ter-nal, bright, and fair; When the saved of Earth shall gath-er o-ver
(2) glo-ry of His res-ur-rec-tion share; When His cho-sen ones shall gath-er to their
(3) talk of all His won-drous love and care; Then when all of life is o-ver and our

Since Jesus Came Into My Heart

Sometimes a heartfelt song can move a stubborn soul. That, at least, is the story George Sanville tells about the gospel hymn, "Since Jesus Came Into My Heart." The song was written by R. H. McDaniel in 1914 and set to music by the famous revivalist music-leader Charles H. Gabriel, just in time to be used for a 3-day soul-gathering meeting in Philadelphia. A certain policeman in attendance by the name of Fowler was resisting the call of the evangelizing preachers with all the Irish stubbornness of his nature. It was not until the final moments of the service when Homer Rodeheaver got up to introduce a new song—this one, which he performed from a freshly printed leaflet—that Fowler finally gave way and was converted. Not only that, but 100 other policemen in the audience followed his lead and were baptized too.

Words by R. H. McDaniel   **Music by Charles H. Gabriel**

(3) I'm possessed of a hope that is steadfast and sure,
Since Jesus came into my heart!
And no dark clouds of doubt now my pathway obscure
Since Jesus came into my heart!
Chorus

(4) There's a light in the valley of death now for me,
Since Jesus came into my heart!
And the gates of the city beyond I can see,
Since Jesus came into my heart!
Chorus

(5) I shall go there to dwell in that city I know,
Since Jesus came into my heart!
And I'm happy, so happy as onward I go,
Since Jesus came into my heart!
Chorus

His Eye Is on the Sparrow

"Why should I feel discouraged?" sang Ethel Waters as the stage lights grew darker bit by bit. Then Julie Harris and Brandon de Wilde joined in singing: "For His eye is on the sparrow, and I know He cares for me." Every night, the second-act curtain of The Member of the Wedding, Carson McCuller's hit drama of 1950, gave the audience a delicious emotional experience. And it gave Ethel Waters the chance to sing a hymn she had known and loved since childhood. Her adored grandmother, whom she called Mom, had loved it too,

and when she lay dying she asked to hear it again. Ethel Waters said she sang it that time like a prayer. "Yes, I still pray before each show," she wrote later in her autobiography (which she entitled His Eye Is on the Sparrow),"only I don't get down on my knees. I've found out that God doesn't mind whether you kneel or sit down or stand up so long as you pray to Him sincerely." This song was popularized by Homer Rodeheaver, colleague and favorite singer of the towering revival evangelist Billy Sunday.

Words by Mrs. C. D. Martin   **Music by Charles H. Gabriel**

(1) Why should I feel dis- cour-aged?___ Why should the shad-ows come?
(2) "Let not thy heart be trou-bled,"___ His ten-der word I hear,
(3) When-ev-er I am tempt-ed,___ When-ev-er clouds a- rise,

(1) Why should my heart be lone-ly___ And long for heav'n and home,___ When
(2) And rest-ing on His good-ness,___ I lose my doubts and fears,___ Tho'
(3) When song gives place to sigh-ing,___ When hope with-in me dies,___ I

Section 5 · Sunday School Favorites

Stand Up, Stand Up for Jesus

"Tell them to stand up for Jesus!" Those were the last words of Dudley Atkins Tyng, a Philadelphia clergyman, as he lay dying on Tuesday, April 13, 1858, the victim of a freak accident. Meanwhile that week the city was in the grip of a triumphant evangelical revival. The following Sunday, one of Tyng's brother ministers, the Rev. George Duffield, preached a magnificent sermon—no doubt inspired by the revival and by Tyng's *inspiriting words—based on this text: "Stand therefore, having your loins girt about with truth." He concluded with some stanzas he had written, titled "Stand Up, Stand Up for Jesus," and shortly thereafter they were published as a broadside, in the fashion of those days. The tune, by George James Webb, fits the text perfectly, although it was written some years earlier to fit a secular poem beginning, "'Tis dawn, the lark is singing. . . ."*

Words by George Duffield   **Music by George James Webb**

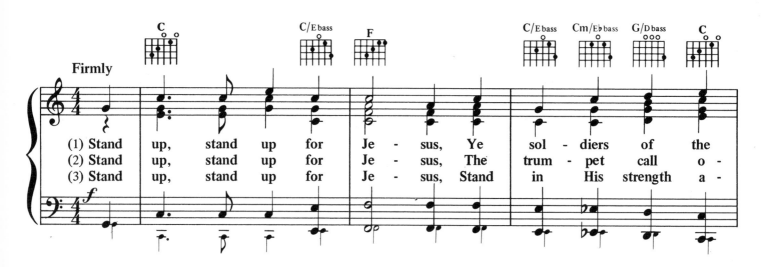

(1) Stand up, stand up for Je-sus, Ye sol-diers of the
(2) Stand up, stand up for Je-sus, The trum-pet call o-
(3) Stand up, stand up for Je-sus, Stand in His strength a-

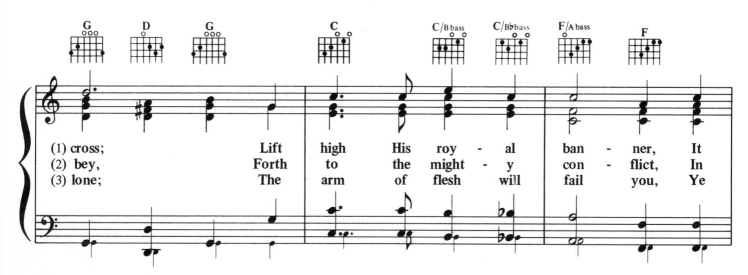

(1) cross;   Lift high His roy-al ban-ner, It
(2) bey,   Forth to the might-y con-flict, In
(3) lone;   The arm of flesh will fail you, Ye

(1) must not suf - fer loss: From vic - t'ry un - to
(2) this His glo - rious day; Ye that are men now
(3) dare not trust your own; Put on the Gos - pel

(1) vic - t'ry, His ar - my shall He lead,_____ Till
(2) serve Him A - gainst un - num - bered foes;_____ Let
(3) ar - mor, Each piece put on with pray'r._____ Where

(1) ev - 'ry foe is van - quished, And Christ is Lord in - deed.
(2) cour - age rise with dan - ger, And strength to strength op - pose.
(3) du - ty calls or dan - ger, Be nev - er want - ing there.

ONWARD, CHRISTIAN SOLDIERS

For the religious holiday of Whitsunday in 1864, an English vicar named Sabine Baring-Gould arranged to have the children of his parish join the children in a nearby village, and he wrote this marching song for them to sing as they walked between the two towns.

The original tune was a slow movement from a Haydn symphony. But the text, published in a religious magazine, attained such popularity that the great Sir Arthur Sullivan, of Gilbert and Sullivan fame, wrote this stirring melody for it in 1871.

Words by Sabine Baring-Gould   **Music by Sir Arthur Sullivan**

(1) On - ward, Chris - tian sol - diers, March - ing as to war,
(2) Like a might - y ar - my Moves the church of God;
(3) On - ward, then, ye peo - ple, Join our hap - py throng,

(1) With the cross of Je - sus Go - ing on be - fore:
(2) Broth - ers, we are tread - ing Where the saints have trod;
(3) Blend with ours your voic - es In the tri - umph song;

(1) Christ the roy - al mas - ter Leads a - gainst the foe;
(2) We are not di - vid - ed, All one bod - y we,
(3) Glo - ry, laud, and hon - or Un - to Christ the King;

Brighten the Corner Where You Are

Words by Ina Duley Ogdon
Music by Charles H. Gabriel

Ina Duley Ogdon's all-embracing wish as a young woman was to join the Chautauqua circuit as an evangelist and bring to thousands her strongly felt message of love and Christian belief. This was in the early days of the 20th century, when gospel meetings were popular, spurring lagging faith with song, personal testimony, and shared experiences. Unfortunately, Mrs. Ogdon's father was an invalid who required constant care; so she abandoned her dreams and reconciled herself to spending her life serving him. Undaunted, she poured out her faith in such songs as "Brighten the Corner Where You Are." When she wrote the lines, "To the many duties ever near you now be true," she could well have been thinking of dishwashing, sweeping, and cleaning, which to her became work God had assigned her, and therefore sacred. Her friend Charles H. Gabriel wrote the music, and Homer Rodeheaver, the famous evangelist, selected it as his theme song. Thus, though she never reached the attention of thousands of people as a Chautauqua speaker, her message has come to millions through music.

(1) Do not wait until some deed of great-ness you may do, Do not wait to shed your light a - far, To the man - y du - ties ev - er near you

(2) (Just a -) bove are cloud - ed skies that you may help to clear, Let not nar - row self your way de - bar; Though in - to one heart a - lone may fall your

(3) (Here for) all your tal - ent you may sure - ly find a need, Here re - flect the bright and morn - ing star; E - ven from your hum - ble hand the bread of

In the Garden

"I seemed to be standing at the entrance to a garden, looking down a gently winding path shaded by olive branches," writes C. Austin Miles of the remarkable experience—almost a trance—that produced this hymn. "A woman in white walked slowly into the shadows. It was Mary. As she came to the tomb, she bent over to look in, and leaning her head upon her arm, she wept. Turning herself, she saw Jesus standing beside her; so did I. I knew it was He. . . ." Miles awakened from his vision at that moment, profoundly moved, inspiration vibrant within him. "I wrote as quickly as the words could be formed the poem exactly as it has since appeared. That same evening I wrote the music." The date was a March day in 1912. Since that memorable time, "In the Garden" has become one of the most beloved of all gospel songs, at once tender and confident, sublimely full of eternal promise.

Words and Music by C. Austin Miles

(1) I come to the gar - den a - lone, While the
(2) (He) speaks, and the sound of His voice Is so
(3) (I'd) stay in the gar - den His with Him Though the

(1) dew is still on the ros - es; And the voice I hear, Fall - ing
(2) sweet the birds hush their sing - ing, And the mel - o - dy That He
(3) night a - round me be fall - ing, But He bids me go; Through the

157

Jesus Loves the Little Children

Perhaps George F. Root is best remembered for some of the songs he wrote during the Civil War ("Tramp! Tramp! Tramp!" and "Just Before the Battle, Mother" are two of them), but his incredibly active life as a musician encompassed many directions. He was interested in church music and hymns from the time he was a boy soprano in a Boston choir until his death in 1895, and he composed many religious songs, usually with texts by others. One of his favorite writers was a Chi-cago preacher named C. H. Woolston. Woolston wrote "Jesus Loves the Little Children" to the tune of Root's "Tramp! Tramp! Tramp!" Today the song is beloved by children and adults alike, and by those of all colors—"red and yellow, black and white," as the song itself puts it, in a surprisingly early show of ecumenicity. The contemporary songwriter Ray Stevens used its refrain as the introduction to his inspirational hit, "Everything Is Beautiful" (page 176).

Words by C. H. Woolston   **Music by George F. Root**

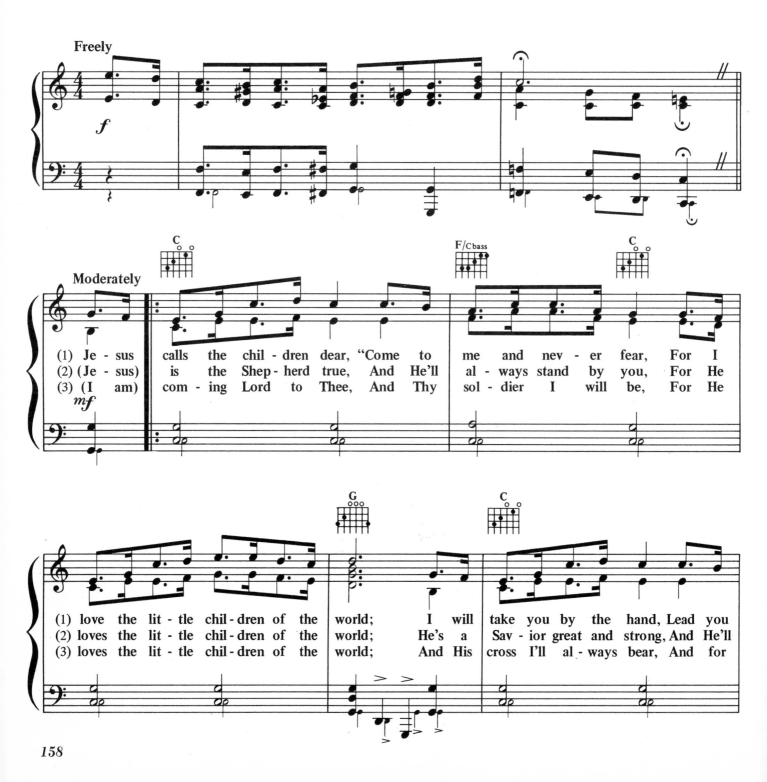

(1) Je - sus calls the chil - dren dear, "Come to me and nev - er fear, For I
(2) (Je - sus) is the Shep - herd true, And He'll al - ways stand by you, For He
(3) (I am) com - ing Lord to Thee, And Thy sol - dier I will be, For He

(1) love the lit - tle chil - dren of the world; I will take you by the hand, Lead you
(2) loves the lit - tle chil - dren of the world; He's a Sav - ior great and strong, And He'll
(3) loves the lit - tle chil - dren of the world; And His cross I'll al - ways bear, And for

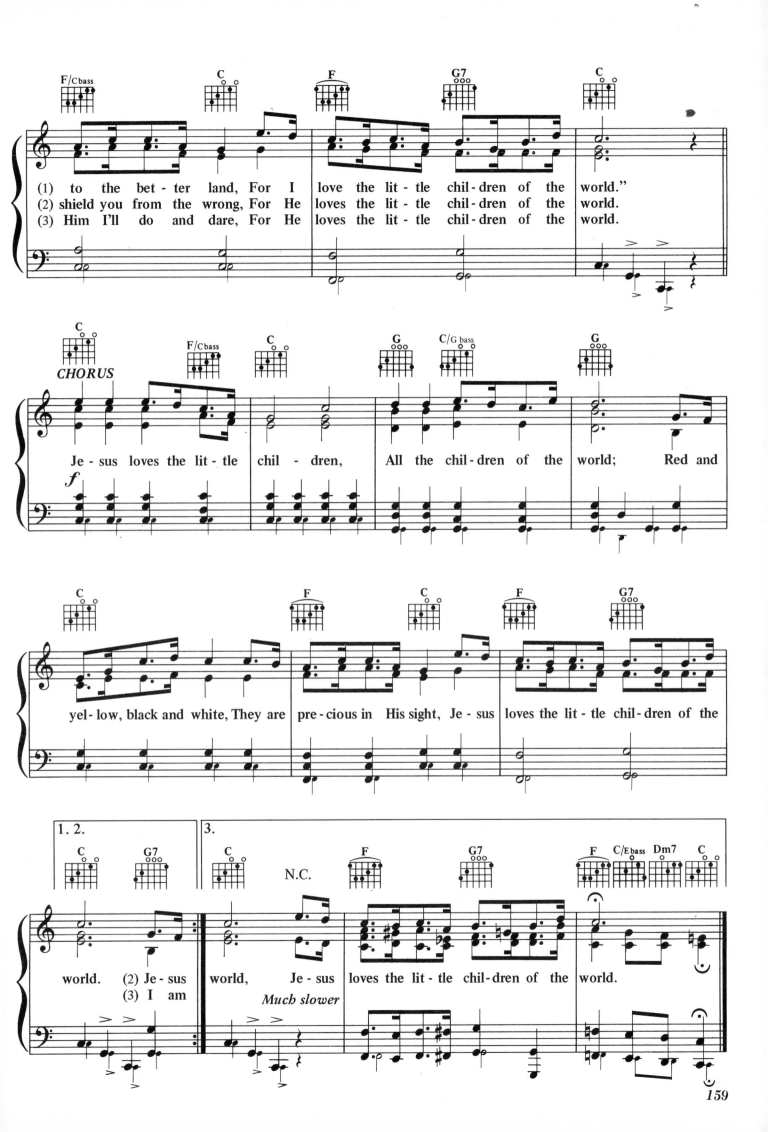

OH HAPPY DAY

Words by Philip Doddridge **Music by E. F. Rimbault**

The poem "Oh Happy Day" was published in 1755, 4 years after its author, Philip Doddridge, a London preacher, died of consumption in Lisbon where he had gone for a rest from overwork. A century later "Oh Happy Day" had become so popular that Queen Victoria's music-loving husband, Prince Albert, requested that it be sung at the confirmations of their children, even though the tune, by E. F. Rimbault, an English organist, seemed to some pious observers to be rather high-spirited for such an august occasion. Yet another century passed, and an American arranger, Edwin Hawkins, came up with a choral bestseller based on this hymn, rooting his version in a black gospel idiom that made it the next best thing to holding a revival meeting right in your own home. For 10 weeks in 1969 the song hovered at the top of the popularity charts, once again familiarizing the words that Reverend Doddridge had based on verses from Psalm 56.

(1) Oh hap-py day that fixed my choice on Thee, my Sav — ior and my
(2) Oh hap-py bond that seals my vows to Him who mer - its all my

God! Well may this glow - ing heart re - joice, And tell its rap - tures all a -
love! Let cheer-ful an - thems fill His house, While to that sa - cred shrine I

CHORUS

G

broad.
move. Hap - py day, hap - py day, When Je - sus washed my sins a -

D7

G

way! He taught me how to watch and pray, And live re - joic - ing ev - 'ry

day; Hap - py day, hap - py day, when Je - sus washed my sins a - way.

D7   G   D.S. %

Slower

(3) 'Tis done: the great transaction's done;
I am my Lord's, and He is mine;
He drew me, and I followed on,
Charmed to confess the voice divine.
Chorus

(4) Now rest my long divided heart;
Fixed on this blissful center rest;
Nor ever from my Lord depart,
With Him of ev'ry good possessed.
Chorus

The Little Brown Church in the Vale

In the town of Bradford, Iowa, pioneers built a rustic church, which they finished and dedicated in 1864, just about Christmastime. All the wood, all the labor, all the love that went into the church as gifts from those sturdy folk made it even then a warm, beckoning kind of place. A minister who lived not far from Bradford, and who had helped with the construction, was so struck by the church's special quality that he wrote a song destined to acquaint all the world with its neighborliness and old-fashioned spirituality. Today more than 40,000 visitors come each year to the little brown church in the vale, so effectively identified in this stirring tune by Dr. William S. Pitts.

Words and Music by William S. Pitts

Moderately and very steady

mf

(1) There's a church in the val - ley by the wild - wood, No
(2) How sweet on a clear Sab - bath morn - ing, To
(3) From the church in the val - ley by the wild - wood when

(1) love - li - er place in the dale; No___ spot is so dear to my
(2) list to the clear ring - ing bell; Its___ tones so sweet - ly are
(3) day fades a - way in - to night, I would fain from this spot of my

*Basses may continue to sing the word "come" on the lowest note of each chord.

163

I LOVE TO TELL THE STORY

Words by Katherine Hankey
Music by William G. Fischer

Katherine Hankey, born to wealth in London, used her resources and her limitless energy to teach the Bible to poor working girls and to assist evangelical groups. While convalescing from an illness, she spent her time composing a long poem on the life of Jesus. One extract from it became known as "I Love To Tell the Story" and was published separately in 1866, with all royalties going to charity. In 1869 William G. Fischer, an American maker of pianos, who frequently led song services for revival meetings, wrote the tune that would make it famous everywhere.

(1) I love to tell the sto - ry, Of un - seen things a -
(2) (I) love to tell the sto - ry, More won - der - ful it

bove, Of Je - sus and His glo - ry, Of Je - sus and His
seems Than all the gold - en fan - cies Of all our gold - en

love. I love to tell the sto - ry, Be - cause I know 'tis
dreams. I love to tell the sto - ry, It did so much for

(3) I love to tell the story,
   'Tis pleasant to repeat,
   What seems each time I tell it
   More wonderfully sweet.
   I love to tell the story,
   For some have never heard
   The message of salvation
   From God's own holy word.
   Chorus

(4) I love to tell the story,
   For those who know it best
   Seem hungering and thirsting
   To hear it like the rest.
   And when, in scenes of glory,
   I sing the new, new song,
   'Twill be the old, old story
   That I have loved so long.
   Chorus and final ending

What a Friend We Have in Jesus

Joseph Scriven, the author of "What a Friend We Have in Jesus," was modest for a writer. He let this hymn (and others) be published in several collections anonymously, and finally when he was given credit for "What a Friend," more than 30 years after it was written in 1855, he attempted to share the honor, saying, "The Lord and I did it between us." Actually he simply meant to compose a few verses for the consolation of his aging mother and never imagined that they would attain such universal recognition. Charles C. Converse, a lawyer, dedicated pipe-organ enthusiast, and the composer of large-scale, serious music, contributed the tune, naming it "Erie" after the Pennsylvania town where he practiced law.

Words by Joseph Scriven   **Music by Charles C. Converse**

(1) What a friend we have in Je - sus, All our sins and griefs to bear,
(2) Have we trials and temp - ta - tions, Is there trou - ble an - y - where?
(3) Are we weak and heav - y la - den, Cum - bered with a load of care?

(1) What a priv - i - lege to car - ry
(2) We should nev - er be dis - cour - aged
(3) Pre - cious Sav - ior still our ref - uge,

166

The Bible Tells Me So

Words and Music by Dale Evans

Dale Evans and her husband, Roy Rogers, were taping a show for their television series in the 1960's when it became apparent that they needed a special song for a tiny girl to sing—a "Sunday school type of song," as Miss Evans put it. "Our producer asked if I could write one very quickly. Behind the closed door of my dressing room on the set, I prayed for the Lord to give me a song. Almost instantly the line 'And now abideth these three: faith, hope, and charity' sprang into my mind, and the rest simply tumbled forth. I went out, sang it, taught it to the little girl, and into the picture it went." "The Bible Tells Me So" was a Hit Parade favorite for many weeks, and of course Dale Evans includes it in nearly all her hundreds of personal appearances.

How do I know? The Bi - ble tells me so._____ Don't

wor - ry 'bout to - mor - row, just be real good to - day. The

Lord is right be - side you, He'll guide you all the way. Have

faith, hope, and char - i - ty,___ That's the way to live suc - cess - ful - ly.___

How do I know? The Bi - ble tells me so._____

HAPPY TRAILS

Words and Music by Dale Evans

Dale Evans wrote "Happy Trails" for the radio show she and her famous cowboy husband, Roy Rogers, had almost a quarter of a century ago. She says, "We have used it in every appearance we have made, publicly, since that time." With its gentle tempo and a melody that seems like a musical echo of the magnificent canyons of the great West, this "till we meet again" song expresses the contentment that an unhurried amble under the friendly open skies can bring.

171

Jesus Wants Me for a Sunbeam

Words by Nellie Talbot   Music by E. O. Excell

Nellie Talbot had run out of lessons for her Sunday school class in a little Missouri church, she recalls, and then rebuked herself for her lack of imagination. "How can you say there's nothing to teach about when you have the sun and the sky and the trees and the flowers!" The lesson she concocted was so attractive that she determined to make it a song. E. O. Excell composed the tune that fits "Jesus Wants Me for a Sunbeam" so buoyantly.

Moderately, with a smile

Je - sus wants me for a sun - beam, To shine for Him each day;
Je - sus wants me to be lov - ing, And kind to all I see;

In ev - 'ry way try to please Him, At home, at school, at play.____
Show - ing how pleas - ant and hap - py His lit - tle one can be.____

CHORUS

sun - beam, a sun - beam, Je - sus wants me for a sun - beam; A

sun - beam, a sun - beam, I'll be a sun - beam for Him.

Put Your Hand in the Hand

Gene MacLellan is a Canadian, one of the country's new breed of talented writer-performers whose reputation has spread worldwide. Still he remains humble, self-effacing, and self-contained, except through his songs, preferring the rustic solitude of Prince Edward Island to Toronto, where he grew up. He has worked in many places—as a busboy, farmer, and hospital attendant; as a rock guitarist and as a musical performer with a traveling evangelist. The fundamentalist part of him, in fact, is as strong as his country and rock influences—it found fruition in this old-fashioned gospel spiritual. Like MacLellan's big country-pop hit of the previous year, "Snowbird," "Put Your Hand in the Hand" was introduced in 1970 by the Canadian superstar Anne Murray. However, the bestselling recording was by Ocean, a black gospel-rock group, on the Buddah label.

Words and Music by Gene MacLellan

EVERYTHING IS BEAUTIFUL

Ray Stevens was always known as a clown, a comedy man. He had been around since 1956, singing zany numbers like "Gitarzan" (in which he took all parts—Tarzan, Jane, and an ape) and recording romantic takeoffs like "Ahab the Arab." So it came as a great surprise when this Georgia lad not only composed the serious and inspirational "Everything Is Beautiful" but went on to sing it so glowingly that his recording was the big top-of-the-popularity-charts winner for the summer of 1970. Other singers took over the song, and in a matter of weeks it entered the realm of the standards.

Words and Music by Ray Stevens

Last time to Coda ⊕

No chords

sum-mer night or a snow-cov-ered win-ter's day. Ev-'ry-bod-y's

beau-ti-ful in their own way, un-der God's

Heav-en the world's gon-na find a way.

There is none so
We should-n't care a-bout the

blind as
length of his hair or the

he who will not
col-or of his

see,
skin,

We must not close our minds, we must let our thoughts be
Don't wor-ry a-bout what shows from with-out but the love that lives with-

177

free.____

in.____

For ev - e - ry hour   that pass - es by____

We gon - na get it all to - geth - er now,

you know the world gets a lit - tle bit old - er.

and ev - 'ry-thing gon - na work out____ fine.____

It's time to re - a - lize____

Just take a lit - tle time____ to

that beau - ty lies in the eyes____

look on the good side my friend

And straight - en it out in your

of the be -

hold - er.____

mind.____

And ev - 'ry-thing is

And ev - 'ry-thing is

N.C.

D.S. % last time to Coda

Coda

178

I'd Like To Teach the World To Sing
(In Perfect Harmony)

Not often do commercial products sponsor songs that prove to be bestsellers, but it was The Coca-Cola Company that gave "I'd Like To Teach the World To Sing" to a world just waiting, apparently, for a chance to warble in perfect harmony. And there is not a single reference to the famous beverage in the lyrics. The New Seekers made the most successful of many recordings, *and in 1971 the song lingered for several weeks at the top of the popularity charts. Then, as smoothly as its promise of "apple trees and honeybees and snow-white turtledoves," "I'd Like To Teach the World To Sing" moved from the ephemeral status of a popular-song hit into lasting popularity, especially as a rousing get-together tune in churches and Sunday schools.*

Words and Music by B. Backer, B. Davis, R. Cook, and R. Greenaway

Let the world sing to - day

song of peace that ech - oes on and nev - er goes a - way.

Put your hand in my hand,

let's be - gin to - day, Put your hand in my

hand, help me find the way. I'd

D.S. %* *to final ending*

I Believe in Music

Words and Music by Mac Davis

"I think music should be for everybody," said Mac Davis, looking down affectionately at his guitar and strumming it idly. It was a quiet moment on his own television show, and he was not sitting on a stage but perched on a makeshift bench right in the middle of his audience. "If we're ever going to talk to each other, let's do it with a song," he continued, unconsciously paraphrasing one of his own songs, "I Believe in Music," published in 1970. "Music is love," the lyrics run, and "Music is the universal language." Davis, a country singer whose career in a few years has exploded like a long-tailed comet, obviously believes what he sings.

With a lilt

(1) Well, I could just sit a-round makin' mu-sic all day long,
(2) Mu-sic is love, love is mu-sic, if you know what I mean,

Long as I'm mak-in' mu-sic, I know I can't
Peo-ple who be-lieve in mu-sic are the hap-pi-est

do no-bod-y wrong. And, who knows, may-be some-day I'll come
peo-ple I ev-er seen. So clap your hands, stomp your feet,

(3) Music is the universal language, and love is the key
To brotherhood and peace and understanding, to livin' in harmony.
So take your brother by the hand, and sing along with me,
And find out what it really means to be young and rich and free.
Chorus and fade

183

DOMINIQUE

French Words and Music by Soeur Sourire, O.P.
English Words by Noël Regney

Soeur Sourire or, to give her her real name, Sister Luc-Gabrielle, served the Dominican order in a convent near the historic Belgian town of Waterloo; there in her moments of quietude she made up little songs for her sister nuns. One of their favorites was "Dominique." Soeur Sourire recorded it at a local studio so that a few copies could be pressed for its admirers. Fortunately some high-level recording men happened to hear it, and factories were soon sending it to record shops everywhere.

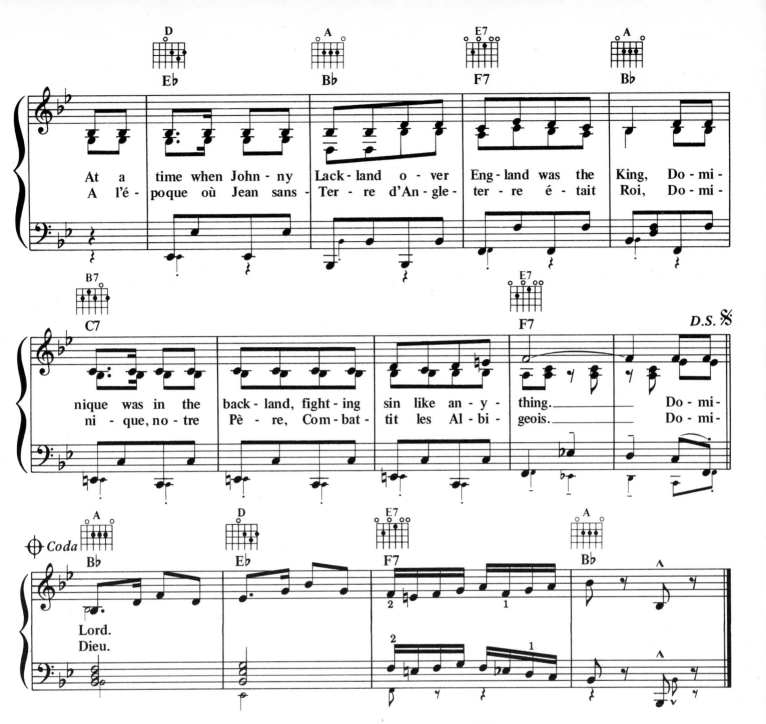

(2) Without horse or fancy wagon, He crossed Europe up and down.
   Poverty was his companion, As he walked from town to town. *Chorus*

(3) To bring back the straying liars And the lost sheep to the fold,
   He brought forth the Preaching Friars, Heaven's soldiers, brave and bold. *Chorus*

(4) One day, in the budding Order, There was nothing left to eat,
   Suddenly two angels walked in With a loaf of bread and meat. *Chorus*

(5) Dominique, once, in his slumber, Saw the Virgin's coat unfurled
   Over Friars without number, Preaching all around the world. *Chorus*

(6) Grant us now, oh Dominique, The grace of love and simple mirth,
   That we all may help to quicken Godly life and truth on earth. *Chorus*

(2) *Ni chameau, ni diligence Il parcourt l'Europe à pied,*
   Scandinavie ou Provence Dans la sainte pauvreté. Refrain

(3) *Enflamma de toute école Filles et garçons pleins d'ardeur,*
   Et pour semer la Parole Inventa Le Frères-Prêcheurs. Refrain

(4) *Chez Dominique et ses frères le pain s'en vint à manquer*
   Et deux anges se présentèrent Portant de grands pains dorés. Refrain

(5) *Dominique vit en rêve Les précheurs du monde entier*
   Sous le manteau de la Vierge En grand nombre rassemblés. Refrain

(6) *Dominique, mon bon Père, Garde-nous simples et gais*
   Pour annoncer a nos frères La Vie et la Verité. Refrain

What the World Needs Now Is Love

Words by Hal David   Music by Burt Bacharach

Burt Bacharach and Hal David wrote "What the World Needs Now" several years before it was used. Then one day in 1968 they found themselves in need of another song for an unfinished recording session. They searched out this number and showed it to singer Dionne Warwicke. She loved it, learned it, and taped it straightaway; thus was one of the top successes of the year born. David remembers writing the lyrics and trying to imagine what the world does not need, what there is already enough of on this earth where too many have too little. As soon as he came to the idea of mountains and oceans and hills—the gifts God has poured out in such abundance—the rest of the song, he says, wrote itself.

No, not just for some,___ but for ev - 'ry - one.___

Lord, we don't need an - oth - er moun - tain,___ There are

moun - tains and hill - sides e - nough to climb;___ There are

o - ceans and riv - ers e - nough to cross,___ E - nough to last

till the end of time.___ What the world needs now is

187

A SONG OF JOY

Beethoven's Ninth Symphony, his last, summed up a monumental life, and there are many who believe that the theme of the last movement is the noblest melody in all his works. Beethoven created this finale for full orchestra with vocal soloists and a large chorus, using as a basis his favorite poem, written by a compatriot, Friedrich von Schiller, and called An die Freude ("Ode to Joy"). The entire symphony has always been played frequently, probably because of the spectacular last movement, but the theme of the finale has always been heard by itself too, sometimes as a hymn tune for words beginning, "Joyful, joyful, we adore Thee." The Beatles used the music in their film Help!. Then in 1970, 200 years after Beethoven's birth, a top Spanish singer, Orbe-Waldo de los Rios, turned the tune into a popular new hit, calling his adaptation "A Song of Joy."

English Words by Ross Parker; Spanish Words and Music by Orbe-Waldo de los Rios

Come sing a song of joy, for peace shall come, my broth - er,___

Sing, sing a song of joy, for men shall love each oth - er.___

That day will dawn just as sure as hearts that are pure are hearts set free. No ___
Reach out and take them in yours with love that en-dures for - ev - er - more. Then ___

___ man must stand a - lone with out - stretched hand be - fore him. ___
___ sing a song of joy for love and un - der - stand - ing. ___

Faster

1.

2.

Guitar tacet

Original tempo

pp

Come sing a song of joy, of free-dom tell the sto-ry,___

Sing, sing a song of joy, for man-kind in his glo-ry.___

cresc.

One might-y voice that will bring a sound that will ring for-ev-er-more. Then___

f

___ sing a song of joy, for love and un-der-stand-ing.___

191

LET IT BE

One of the last collaborations between Beatles John Lennon and Paul McCartney was "Let It Be," written, according to McCartney, especially for soul singer Aretha Franklin. The song is based on one line of a mellow old New Orleans gospel hymn, "Just a Closer Walk With Thee," and endowed with a truly devotional melody. The melody is akin to many hit songs of the early 1970's, when a flood of popular tunes based on religion and brotherhood filled the airwaves.

Words and Music by John Lennon and Paul McCartney

Additional Words

And when the night is cloudy, there is still a light that shines on me,
Shine until tomorrow, let it be.
I wake up to the sound of music, Mother Mary comes to me,
Speaking words of wisdom, let it be.

Let it be, let it be, let it be, let it be
There will be an answer, let it be.
Let it be, let it be, let it be, let it be,
There will be an answer, let it be.

ALL YOU NEED IS LOVE

Like all singing groups in the late 1960's, the Beatles turned finally to love for some of their finest songs, having exhausted more ironical subjects like meter maids, Norwegian wood, and Buffalo Bill. Their beat became solemn, their sentiment became sincere, and in 1967 John Lennon and Paul McCartney wrote "All You Need Is Love." Its theme of peace was a welcome one during those years of strain and remains so, as the song's slow but constant growth in popularity gives evidence.

Words and Music by

John Lennon and

Paul McCartney

I Will Never Pass This Way Again

In a musing, declamatory style, Ronnie Gaylord gives us a poetic song that pleads for the importance of today's opportunities. "I Will Never Pass This Way Again" was written in 1972, but the message is a familiar and timeless one: Do the good that you can do, today; tomorrow may be too late to reach out to those who need you. The song has both an echo of the tempo of soft rock and the simplicity of folk music, but its roots are in the old-time spiritual. This is most obvious in its "soul" refrain: "Oh Lord, please show me how!"

Words and Music by Ronnie Gaylord

Slowly, with expression

I will pass this way but once.

If there's an-y good that I can do, let me do it now,

for I'll nev-er pass this way a-gain. I will see this day but

If We Only Have Love

A spectacularly successful 1968 off-Broadway revue in New York called Jacques Brel Is Alive and Well and Living in Paris brought the song-writing genius of that Frenchman to a wide public in this country for the first time. Since the mid-1950's, however, when songs like "If We Only Have Love" were written, his super-Gallic sentiment and subtlety had won discerning friends.

Brel, indeed alive and very successful in Paris, composes both music and words. He sings his songs in a muted, intimate fashion that enhances their romantic quality. Something of that same style infused two bestselling recordings of this song—those of Dionne Warwicke and Johnny Mathis—which featured English lyrics by Mort Shuman and Eric Blau.

French Words and Music by Jacques Brel   **English Words by Mort Shuman and Eric Blau**

(1) Quand on n'a que l'amour
    A s'offrir en partage
    Au jour du grand voyage,
    Qu'est notre grand amour;
    Quand on n'a que l'amour,
    Mon amour, toi et moi,
    Pour qu'éclatent de joie
    Chaque heure et chaque jour;
    Quand on n'a que l'amour
    Pour vivre nos promesses
    Sans nulle autre richesse
    Que d'y croire toujours;
    Quand on n'a que l'amour
    Pour meubler de merveilles
    Et couvrir de soleil
    La laideur des faubourgs;
    Quand on n'a que l'amour
    Pour unique raison
    Pour unique chanson
    Et unique secours;

(2) Quand on n'a que l'amour
    A offrir en prière
    Pour les maux de la terre,
    En simple troubadour;
    Quand on n'a que l'amour
    Pour habiller matin,
    Pauvres et malandrins,
    De manteaux de velours;
    Quand on n'a que l'amour
    A offrir à ceux-là,
    Dont l'unique combat
    Est de chercher le jour;
    Quand on n'a que l'amour
    Pour tracer un chemin
    Et forcer le destin
    A chaque carrefour;
    Quand on n'a que l'amour
    Pour parler aux canons
    Et rien qu'une chanson
    Pour convaincre un tambour;

Extension de seconde stance
Alors, sans avoir rien
Que la force d'aimer,
Nous aurons dans nos mains,
Ma mie, le monde entier.

203

Put a Little Love in Your Heart

**Words and Music by Jimmy Holiday,
Randy Myers, and Jackie de Shannon**

Jackie de Shannon coauthored the song for which she is so widely known as a performer—"Put a Little Love in Your Heart"—and in April of 1969 she sang it to the top of the popularity charts. First making her talent known in 1964 as one of the warm-up acts on the staggeringly successful coast-to-coast American tour of The Beatles, she won further praise when she added Bob Dylan's then-new songs to her repertoire. More fundamental than The Beatles, more vigorous than Dylan, "Put a Little Love in Your Heart" is her own special plea for happiness through brotherhood, set to a gospel-rock beat.

(1) Think of your fel - low man, lend him a help - ing hand,
(2) An - oth - er day goes by, and still the chil - dren cry,
(3) Take a good look a - round, and if you're look - in' down,

(1) Put a lit - tle love in your heart.
(2) Put a lit - tle love in your heart.
(3) Put a lit - tle love in your heart. If

(1) You see, it's get - ting late, oh, please don't hes - i - tate,
(2) you want the world to know, we won't let ha - tred grow,
(3) I hope when you de - cide, kind - ness will be your guide,

204

Section 7 · Favorites of the Folksingers

TURN! TURN! TURN!
(To Everything There Is a Season)

Taking his text almost verbatim from the third chapter of the Book of Ecclesiastes, Pete Seeger in 1962 wrote a song about the harmonious balance of life that he called "Turn! Turn! Turn!" (That refrain is the only part of the lyrics that is not Biblical in origin.) The song became one of the best known compositions of this acknowledged authority on folksong, whose father was also an ethnomusicologist. At the age of 16, Seeger was taken to a folk festival in Asheville, North Carolina, and that experience prompted him to use his education and background in pursuing the indigenous song of this country. Traveling with folksong pioneer Leadbelly and working with such early practitioners of the art as Lee Hays and Woody Guthrie, Seeger finally crystallized his personal feelings about folk art in the late 1960's when he had his own television program. By then folk singers had found an honored place among performers across the land.

Words From the Book of Ecclesiastes **Adaptation and Music by Pete Seeger**

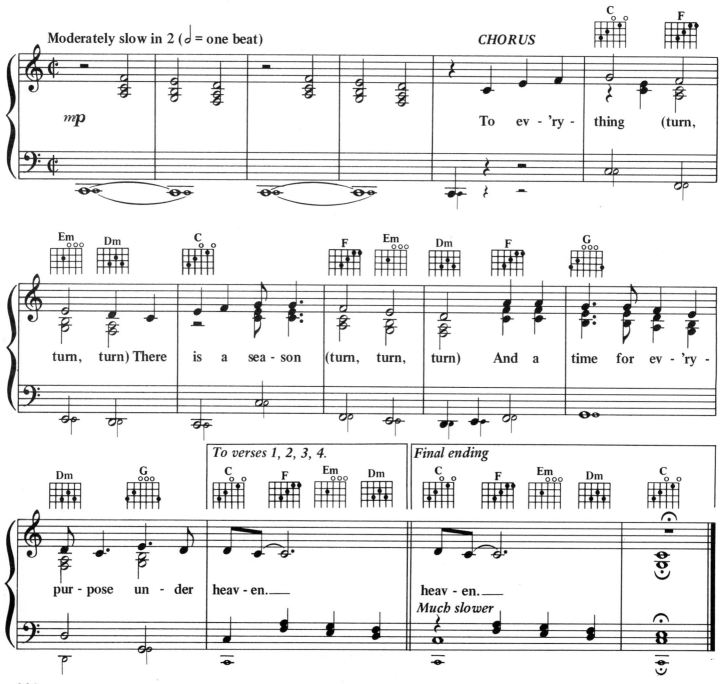

207

KUM BA YA

Nigeria, whose beautiful coastline is washed by the waters of the Gulf of Guinea, was Christianized by European missionaries in the early 19th century. The people of this African country combined the natural dignity of their own folk music with the wonderful news of the Lord's presence and the serene warmth of their carefree climate. Lorraine Hansberry used one beautifully and instantly communicative Nigerian folksong in her play, A Raisin in the Sun. Another somewhat like it is "Kum Ba Ya," translated approximately as "Come by here," which was made particularly popular in Norman Luboff's choral setting for his own choir. Like a chant, the song in succeeding stanzas invokes the Lord to be present as somebody sings, somebody cries, somebody prays.

Kum ba ya, my Lord, Kum ba ya. Kum ba ya, my Lord, Kum ba
Some-one's sing-ing, Lord, Kum ba ya. Some-one's sing-ing, Lord, Kum ba

ya. Kum ba ya, my Lord, Kum ba ya.
ya. Some-one's sing-ing, Lord, Kum ba ya. Oh Lord, Kum ba ya.

You can add your own verses to this song. Some examples:

Someone's crying, Lord
Someone's praying,
Someone's learning,
Someone's hoping,
Someone's working,
Someone's playing,
etc.

If I Had a Hammer

(The Hammer Song)

**Words and Music
by Lee Hays and Pete Seeger**

Lee Hays and Pete Seeger, pioneers in the folk-singing renaissance of the 1930's and 1940's, introduced "If I Had a Hammer" to black students in the Southern Freedom Schools, challenging them then as they do us today to strike with the hammer of justice, to ring the bell of freedom, and to sing the song of love between brothers. Later Seeger, who has been called "the Johnny Appleseed of American folk-song," joined a folk group known as The Weavers, and in 1958 they finally recorded "If I Had a Hammer." Its runaway successes however came several years after that when Peter, Paul, and Mary made a bestselling folk-style record and Trini Lopez did a jubilant, somewhat Latin-styled version.

*Guitarists: Tune lowest string to D.

AMAZING GRACE

Words by John Newton

John Newton never really thought of himself as a poet but rather as a sea captain turned to God. His conversion took place in the midst of a wildly fierce storm at sea; somehow in calming a terror-stricken crew and looking after a piteous horde of African slaves that were his cargo, he found the peace of God. When the storm subsided, the 23-year-old captain made a decision: no more sailing, no more slaving. And after 16 years of studying at night, for he had had no education, religious or otherwise, he was ordained a minister and preached the gospel of love and freedom in word and example. He decorated his colorful sermons with verse, and ultimately he published nearly 300. "Amazing Grace" is the best known. The words, with a melody that may have evolved in the rural southern United States, were sung by folk singers, and a recording by the Royal Scots Dragoon Guards Band, complete with bagpipe solo, was a hit in 1972.

(3) Through many dangers, toils, and snares
   I have already come;
   'Tis grace hath brought me safe thus far,
   And grace will lead me home.
(4) How sweet the name of Jesus sounds
   In a believer's ear;

It soothes his sorrows, heals his wounds,
   And drives away his fear.
(5) Must Jesus bear the cross alone
   And all the world go free?
   No, there's a cross for ev'ryone,
   And there's a cross for me.

WE SHALL OVERCOME

New Words and Music Arrangement by Zilphia Horton
Frank Hamilton, Guy Carawan, and Pete Seeger

Music is an inspiration when the battle is raging. In one form or another, "We Shall Overcome" has provided leadership since the 1940's when striking Southern tobacco workers rallied to its call in their fight for union rights. Neither the verses nor the music, a modified black gospel song, have a clear-cut history. Part of the tune seems to be a close copy of a familiar church song, a Sicilian mariners' hymn; part of it is claimed by *Roberta Martin of Chicago, who published her "I'll Be Like Him Someday" under a pseudonym in 1945, using music very like "We Shall Overcome." But it was Pete Seeger who adopted the title we use today when he included the stirring melody in his recitals of folksongs. The tune has become the unofficial hymn of the black civil rights movement in the United States and in the apartheid-ridden sections of South Africa as well.*

(3) We are not afraid, we are not afraid.
    We are not afraid today,
    etc.

(4) We shall stand together, we shall stand together,
    We shall stand together – now,
    etc.

(5) The truth will make us free, the truth
    will make us free.
    The truth will make us free someday.
    etc.

(6) The Lord will see us through, the Lord
    will see us through.
    The Lord will see us through someday.
    etc.

(7) We shall be like Him, we shall be like Him,
    We shall be like Him someday,
    etc.

(8) We shall live in peace, we shall live in peace.
    We shall live in peace someday.
    etc.

Because All Men Are Brothers

(The Whole Wide World Around)

The titan of baroque composers, Johann Sebastian Bach, based the congregation's portion of his "Passion According to Saint Matthew" on an old Lutheran hymn by Hans Leo Hassler. Two hundred years later Tom Glazer selected the same superb melody for a song about brotherhood, and a folk-singing group called The Weavers picked up "Because All Men Are Brothers" and recorded it. Soon afterward Peter, Paul, and Mary featured the song for a year in their concerts and television performances. Today it appears in the hymnals of Unitarians, Roman Catholics, Lutherans, Presbyterians, the YMCA, and the Quakers. As Glazer himself puts it, "Brotherhood apparently is ecumenical, which, in a troubled world, pleases me very much indeed."

Music by Hans Leo Hassler and Johann Sebastian Bach
Music Adaptation and Words by Tom Glazer

(1) Be- cause all men are broth- ers, Wher- ev- er men may be, One u- nion shall u- nite us For- ev- er proud and free. No

(2) (My) broth- ers are all oth- ers, For- ev- er hand in hand; Where chimes the bell of free- dom, There is my na- tive land. My

(3) (Let) ev- 'ry voice be thun- der, Let ev- 'ry heart be strong, Un- til all ty- rants per- ish, Our work shall not be done. Let

The Wayfaring Stranger

At the beginning of the 19th century there was a mighty religious revival in Kentucky, Tennessee, and the Carolinas, and it was then that a particularly beautiful white spiritual, "Poor Wayfaring Stranger," began to be popularly sung. Some say it was chanted as a solo by penitent souls in the prayer meetings. The song was modeled on a secular English ballad, "The Dear Companion," and in turn influenced a black spiritual, "Pilgrim's Song." Finally this song appeared in print under its present title in The Sacred Harp, a volume of shape-note, or fasola, tunes published in 1844. (Fasola is so called from the symbols for various notes—such as fa, sol, and la—each of which had a different shape to facilitate congregational reading.) The pathetic and personal quality of the tune endeared it to many folksingers who began to revive interest in such music a hundred years later. Burl Ives was one of these, and he used "The Wayfaring Stranger" as the name for his very successful radio show devoted to America's native music and later for his autobiography.

Slowly

(1) I am a poor way-far-ing stran-ger,___ A-wan-d'ring through this world of
(2) I feel my sins are all for-giv-en, My hopes are stayed on things a-

woe, There is no sick-ness,___ no toil, nor dan-ger,___ In that bright
bove, I'm goin' a-way___ to you, bright Heav-en,___ Where all is

world to which I go. }
joy and peace and love. } I'm go-ing there to meet my

(3) I know dark clouds will gather 'round me,
I know my way is rough and steep,
But beauteous fields lie just before me,
Where souls redeemed, their vigil keep.
I'm going there to meet my Savior,
I'm going there to see my Lord.
I'm only going over Jordan,
I'm only going over home.

(4) I want to sing salvation's story,
I'm going with that blood-washed band,
I want to wear a crown of glory,
When I get home to that bright land.
I'm going there to meet my Savior,
I'm going there to see my Lord.
I'm only going over Jordan,
I'm only going over home.

Keep on the Sunny Side

Written by A. P. Carter, "Keep on the Sunny Side" became a trademark of the unique Carter Family, one of the most honored and beloved groups in country music. One day A. P., his wife, Sara, and her cousin, Maybelle, who sang for church socials and weddings, noticed an advertisement for auditions in the Bristol, Tennessee, newspaper. They arrived there from their home in Virginia on August 1, 1927, sang for a representative of the Victor Record Company, and that very day made several recordings that immediately put them into the musical limelight. Country-music lovers had always appreciated them, but suddenly musicologists and sociologists were full of their praises. "Keep on the Sunny Side" is one of many hits that made the Carters known as "Country Music's Royal Family," leading to their permanent place in Nashville's Country Music Hall of Fame.

Words and Music by A. P. Carter and Gary Garett

(1) There's a dark and trou - bled side of life, One that's filled with
(2) (When life's) storm - y, let faith a - bide, And you'll al - ways
(3) (Just re -) mem - ber to sing out strong, When you find the

(1) care and strife, Then the side that plays a hap - py
(2) turn the tide, Light your hopes and you'll come smil - in'
(3) road is long, And your bur - den won't be hard to

221

Keep on the sun-ny side of life;_____ It will help you ev-'ry day, It will bright-en all the way, If you keep on the sun-ny side of

1.
life._____

(2) When life's
(3) Just re -

2.
life._____

8va lower

Jacob's Ladder

Scholars say that "Jacob's Ladder," based on Jacob's vision in the Book of Genesis and originally a white spiritual, was transformed by black slaves into the version that remains so beloved today. This bears out the view of folksong authority Alan Lomax that "where the Negroes took the white hymns they did not copy them; rather they touched them with magic and transformed them into eternal works of art."

(3) Sinner, do you love my Jesus? . . .

(4) If you love Him, why not serve Him? . . .

(5) We are climbing higher, higher. . .

(6) We are climbing Jacob's ladder. . .

THIS TRAIN

In spirituals there are many ways to get to heaven. You can climb Jacob's ladder, or you can cross over a rolling river to the beatitude on the other side. The excitement over the development of the locomotive in North America led to the possibility that you could also take a train to salvation. Your ticket for the ride on the express for glory could be ensured by doing good and eschewing such tempting vices as gambling, lying, hypocrisy, and loose women. With a rhythmic pulse that races like a roaring engine, "This Train," a mid-19th-century spiritual, makes righteousness sound peppier than ever before.

Brightly

G

(1) This train is bound for glo - ry, this train,_____
(2) This train don't carry no gam - blers, this train,_____

D

This train is bound for glo - ry, this train,_____
This train don't carry no gam - blers, this train,_____

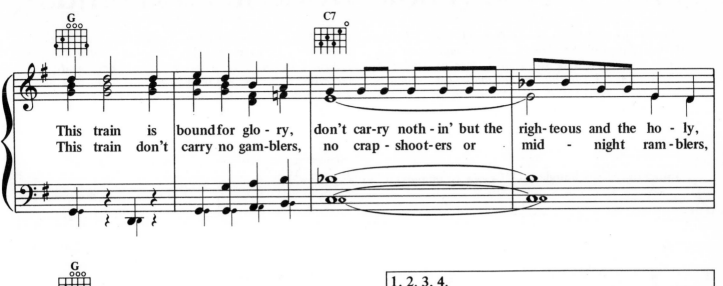

This train is   bound for glo - ry,   don't car-ry noth - in' but the   righ - teous and the ho - ly,
This train don't   carry no gam-blers,   no crap - shoot-ers or   mid - night ram - blers,

1. 2. 3. 4.

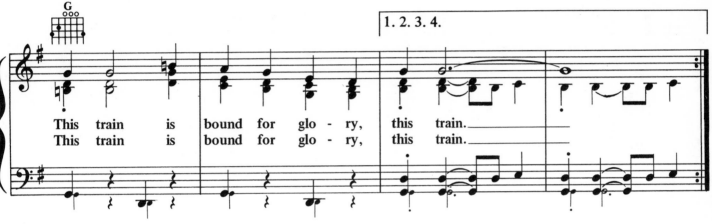

This   train   is   bound   for   glo - ry,   this   train.____
This   train   is   bound   for   glo - ry,   this   train.____

5.

this   train,   this   train,   this   train.

Fading out and slowing down

(3) This train is built for speed, now, *etc.*
    Fastest train you ever did see.
    This train is bound for glory, this train.

(4) This train don't carry no liars, *etc.*
    No hypocrites and no high flyers.
    This train is bound for glory, this train.

(5) This train don't carry no rustlers, *etc.*
    Side-street walkers, two-bit hustlers.
    This train is bound for glory, this train... this train... this train.

He's Got the Whole World in His Hands

One of the first great interpreters of "He's Got the Whole World in His Hands" was the magnificent contralto of concert and opera fame, Marian Anderson. The song was invariably the one audiences wanted to hear when she went all over the world on her State Department-sponsored good-will tours. Then in the *early 1950's Mahalia Jackson brought her own version of the song to her vast gospel following. And in 1958, Laurie London, a 13-year-old English boy, made a recording that was very popular among young and old pop music aficionados. The song is 150 years old, though it was apparently first published in 1927.*

Go Down, Moses

"Go Down, Moses" was the first Negro spiritual, which is still popularly sung today, to be published. In October of 1861 the words appeared in The National Anti-Slavery Standard, a weekly journal, and were said to have been sung at a prayer meeting at Fortress Monroe (where Jefferson Davis was later imprisoned). Then in December the song was issued in sheet music and called "O! Let My People Go"—supposedly sung by the "contrabands," those blacks who had escaped to the Union lines. Spirituals often set down in music the Old Testament stories of tribulation and slavery; the plight of the Israelites under the heavy yoke of Egyptian rule took on the same meaning as the injustice accorded African blacks in their enslavement. Some scholars have even suggested that the spirituals' somber melodies bear a resemblance to ancient Jewish chants.

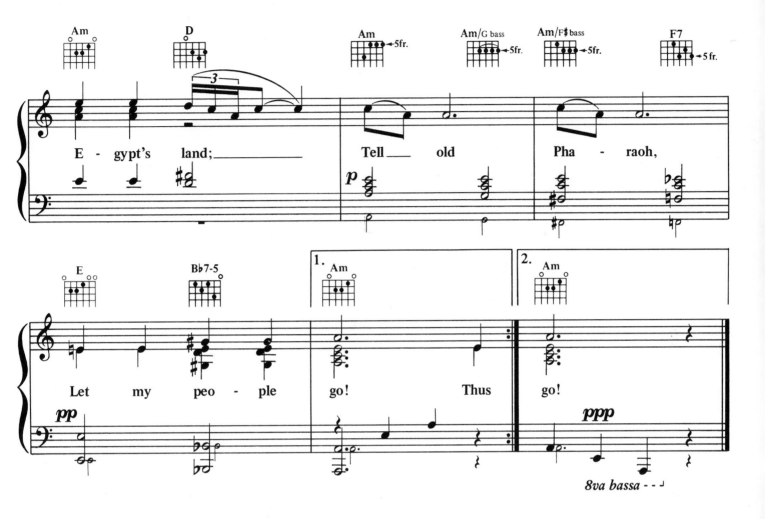

(3) No more shall they in bondage toil,
Let my people go.
Let them come out with Egypt's spoil.
Let my people go.
Chorus

(4) Oh, Moses, the cloud shall cleave the way,
Let my people go.
A fire by night, a shade by day.
Let my people go.
Chorus

(5) Your foes shall not before you stand,
Let my people go.
And you'll possess fair Canaan's land.
Let my people go.
Chorus

WADE IN THE WATER

Wading in the water means being baptized, according to old slave jargon. The evangelistic churches considered that that rite ideally should be performed as St. John the Baptist did it in the River Jordan—by total immersion. For this ancient spiritual there is traditionally a leader and a chorus. The former "lines out" various references to Biblical happenings and to the diffi-culties of finding peace on this earth—not to mention meeting Judgment in the next—while the chorus punctuates his words with the repeated "Wade in the water, children." When Africans were brought to the United States as slaves, they could express their feelings only in song, and with their melodies of enormous emotional range they created a powerful image in music.

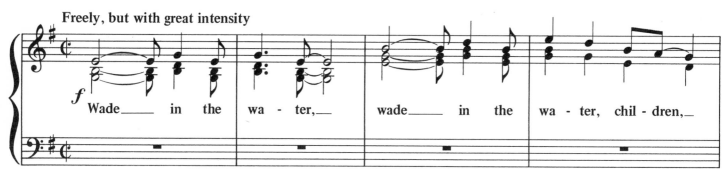

Wade in the water, wade in the water, chil-dren,

Organ pedal tacet till verse

Wade in the water, 'cause God's goin' to trou-ble the wa - ter.

Moderately slow 2 (𝅝 = 1 beat)

This Little Light of Mine

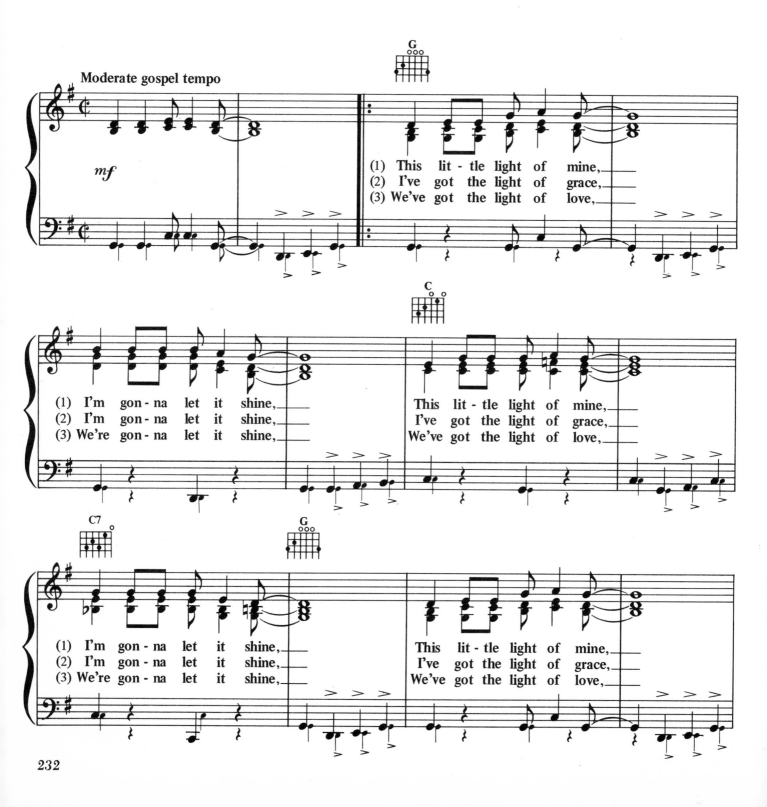

Moderate gospel tempo

mf

G

(1) This lit - tle light of mine,
(2) I've got the light of grace,
(3) We've got the light of love,

(1) I'm gon - na let it shine,
(2) I'm gon - na let it shine,
(3) We're gon - na let it shine,

This lit - tle light of mine,
I've got the light of grace,
We've got the light of love,

C7   **G**

(1) I'm gon - na let it shine,
(2) I'm gon - na let it shine,
(3) We're gon - na let it shine,

This lit - tle light of mine,
I've got the light of grace,
We've got the light of love,

Most spirituals are based on an incident or a verse in the Bible. This one paraphrases two verses from Matthew 5 ("You are the light of the world" and "Let your light so shine before men, that they may see your good works") and one from John 1 ("the true light that enlightens every man was coming into the world"). There have been several popular adaptations that have retained the original gospel rhythm and fervor, particularly Ray Charles' 1955 hit "This Little Girl of Mine," also recorded in 1958 by the Everly Brothers.

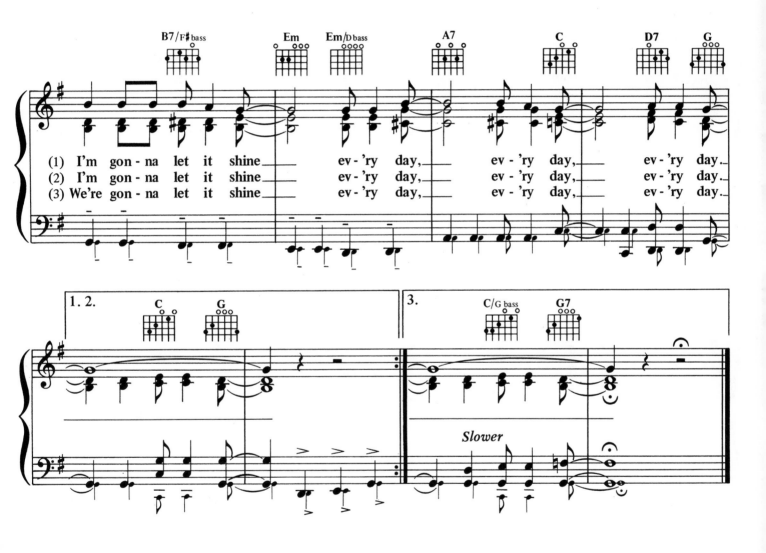

(1) I'm gon - na let it shine___ ev - 'ry day,___ ev - 'ry day,___ ev - 'ry day.
(2) I'm gon - na let it shine___ ev - 'ry day,___ ev - 'ry day,___ ev - 'ry day.
(3) We're gon - na let it shine___ ev - 'ry day,___ ev - 'ry day,___ ev - 'ry day.

Ev'ry Time I Feel the Spirit

"Ev'ry Time I Feel the Spirit" is a "shout" spiritual, full of the exhilaration that the combination of singing and praying gave to so many in the revival meetings of the early 20th century. Even back in 1867 the Nation observed: "The true 'shout' takes place on Sundays or on praise-nights, either in the praise-house or in some cabin in which a regular religious meeting has been held. All stand in the middle of the floor, and the 'sperchil' is struck up. Song and dance are extremely energetic, and when the shout lasts into the middle of the night, the thud-thud of the feet prevents sleep within half a mile of the praise-house." Such energy pervades "Ev'ry Time I Feel the Spirit" with its naive idealism, its restless syncopation, and its confident message: "But while God leads me I'll never fear, for I am sheltered by His care."

last time, end here

spir - it,_____ Mov - in' in my heart,_____ I will pray._____

VERSE

(1) Up - on the moun - tain_____ when my Lord spoke,_____ Out of His
(2) Oh, I have sor - rows_____ and I have woe,_____ And I have

mouth came_____ fire and smoke._____ Look'd all a - round me, It look'd so
heart - ache_____ here be - low;_____ But while God leads me,_ I'll nev - er

D.S. 𝄋

fine,_____ Till I asked my Lord_____ if all were mine._____
fear,_____ For I am shel - tered_____ by His care._____

235

WERE YOU THERE?

Of all spirituals perhaps the most moving is "Were You There?" It exhibits the simple dignity, the infinite tenderness, and the poignancy that have made the spiritual, in the words of one writer, "the finest distinctive artistic contribution America has to offer the world." We are not sure whether this one was originally a white or a black spiritual. There is a version that originated in the all-white upper Cumberland region of Tennessee, but it was never printed. From the Deep South comes this superb black song that was already part of our folklore three or four generations ago. (It was finally published in Old Plantation Hymns, in 1899.) Its profound sorrow, its sense of personal loss—expressed so long ago by an unknown Negro slave—still breathe a spirit of deep religious strength and expectation.

Somewhat freely

mf

F   C7   F   B♭/F bass

(1) Were you there when they cru - ci - fied my Lord? (Were you
(2) (Were you) there when they nailed Him to the Cross? (Were you
(3) (Were you) there when they laid Him in the tomb? (Were you

F   B♭/F bass   F

(1) there?) Were you there when they cru - ci - fied my
(2) there?) Were you there when they nailed Him to the
(3) there?) Were you there when they laid Him in the

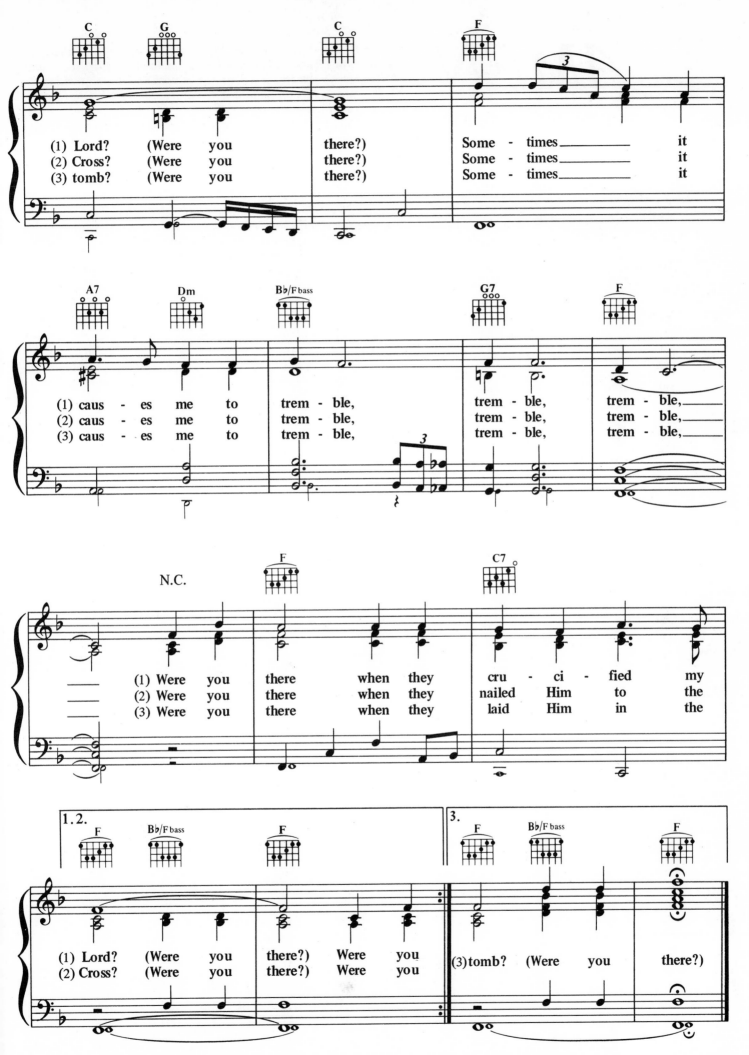

AMEN

Jester Hairston's professional life extends in many directions. He is, to begin, a classically trained musician whose compositions and arrangements, mostly based on Afro-American folksongs and spirituals, earned him an honorary doctorate. The U. S. State Department has sent him as a good-will ambassador to Africa and Europe on five occasions. He also acts on television and in films. His Broadway career started in 1930 with a show called Hello, Paris. But he is perhaps best known as a conductor of choral groups (including, in the 1930's, the then world-famous Hall Johnson Choir). "Amen" dates from 1957. Many became aware of this contagious participation piece when it was sung by a group of German Catholic nuns and Sydney Poitier, who was their black Baptist benefactor, in the moving 1963 film, Lilies of the Field. The picture was nominated for an Oscar, and Poitier's unforgettable performance won him the Academy Award for best actor of the year—the first time this all-important Oscar went to a black.

Words and Music by Jester Hairston

*For easier playing, leader's vocalization may be omitted when playing keyboards.

238

Additional Words (*Leader*)

(2) See Him at the Jordan,
Where John was baptizin'
And savin' all the sinners.
See Him at the seaside,
Talkin' to the fishermen
And makin' them disciples.

(3) Marchin' in Jerusalem
Over palm branches
In pomp and splender.
See Him in the garden,
Prayin' to His Father
In deepest sorrow.

(4) Led before Pilate,
Then they crucified Him,
But He rose on Easter.
Hallelujah,
He died to save us,
And He lives forever.

When the Saints Go Marching In

Very possibly "When the Saints Go Marching In," the most famous of all Dixieland jazz tunes, originated in the Bahamas, and it is possible too that the song was based on a much earlier inspirational tune called "When the Saints March In for Crowning." In any case its pep and its famous "echo" made it popular among the hymn-shouting revivalists at the turn of the century. Early jazz musicians of New Orleans then felt free to throw caution to the winds and did what they pleased with this song, which had already been turned into a

red-hot gospel tune. Some say "The Saints" took on its special flavor because it was used as a funeral march in New Orleans; a hired brass band would accompany the coffin to the cemetery, playing the spiritual with dignity and muffled drums, and then march back to the city playing it in a brightly swinging tempo about twice as fast. The tune became an important part of the musical score for a film, The Green Pastures, in 1936, and in the mid-1940's attained a new audience thanks to the efforts of the old New Orleans trumpeter Bunk Johnson.

240

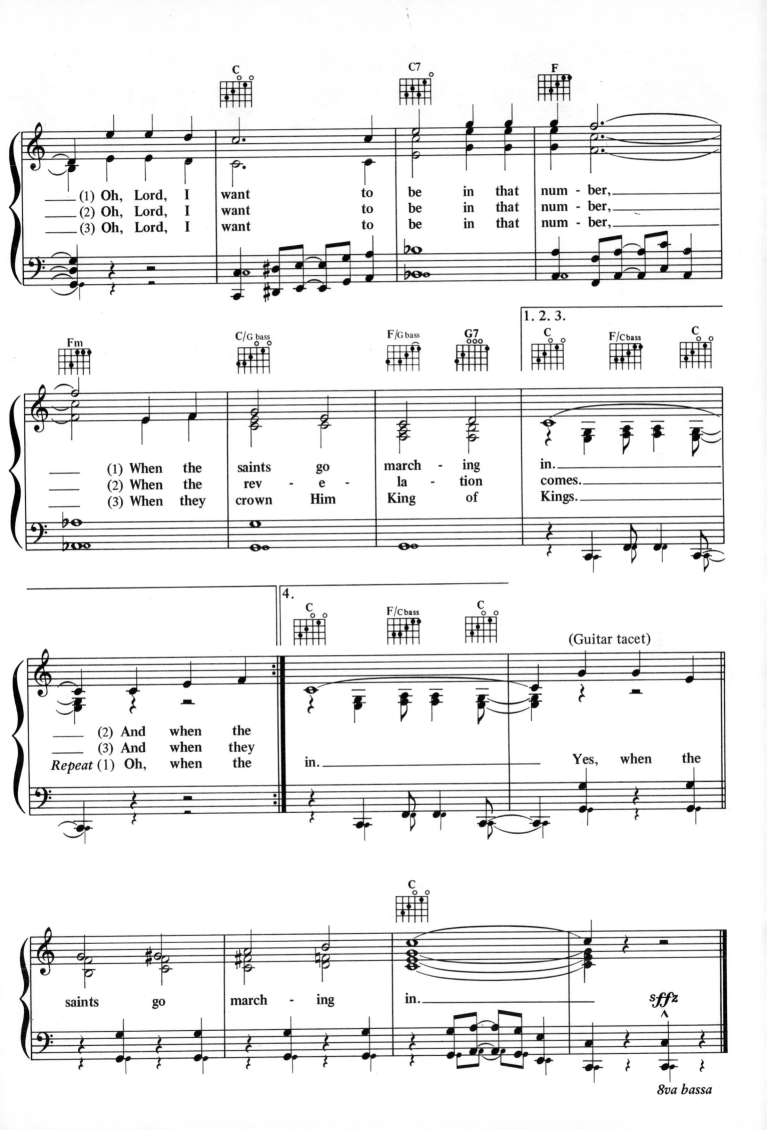

Precious Memories

Tennessee Ernie Ford helped repopularize the oldtime favorite "Precious Memories." He calls it a kind of "Southern-Western spiritual," probably because of its plain but plaintive melody and its four-square harmonies. J. B. F. Wright wrote both the words and music. His memories, which he calls "unseen angels," evoke a mother and a father who made his home a joyful, reverent source of strength that still comforts him over the many years that have passed since his childhood. In the refrain there is a reminiscence of certain favorite spirituals, made more poignant by the expressive musical turn on the word "soul."

Words and Music by J. B. F. Wright

Pre - cious mem - 'ries, un - seen an - gels,
Pre - cious fa - ther, lov - ing moth - er,

Sent from some - where to my soul;
Fly a - cross the lone - ly years;

How they lin - ger,
And old home scenes

243

Sweet Hour of Prayer

Words by William W. Walford
Music by William Batchelder Bradbury

"Sweet Hour of Prayer," by a blind English shopkeeper and occasional preacher named William W. Walford, was printed in 1845. The words caught the eye of a very industrious church composer named William Batchelder Bradbury, who had once been a student in the celebrated Lowell Mason's singing classes in Boston. Like the other works in the more than 50 songbooks this widely known composer published, "Sweet Hour of Prayer" exhibits the transition Bradbury helped make from the sterner, more classic hymn tunes of his mentor, Mason, to the newer, freer, more gospel-like tunes that were soon to surround the religious faith of turn-of-the-century America with a garland of popular melody.

(1) Sweet hour of prayer, sweet hour of prayer, That calls me from a
(2) (Sweet) hour of prayer, sweet hour of prayer, Thy wings shall my pe-
(3) (Sweet) hour of prayer, sweet hour of prayer, May I Thy con-so-

(1) world of care And bids me, at my Fa-ther's throne, Make
(2) ti-tion bear To Him whose truth and faith-ful-ness En-
(3) la-tion share, Till from Mount Pis-gah's loft-y height I

(1) all my wants and wish-es known! In sea-sons of dis-
(2) gage the wait-ing soul to bless; And since He bids me
(3) view my home and take my flight; This robe of flesh I'll

Just a Closer Walk With Thee

Kenneth Morris' setting of "Just a Closer Walk With Thee" seems more like a folksong than a specific composition, and its style makes it seem more like a gospel tune than a folksong. The stately tempo and chromatic melody made it a natural choice for the funeral marches that New Orleans jazz bands used to create so picturesquely when they were hired for such occasions around the turn of the century. Some time later country singer Red Foley recorded a version of the song that turned into one of his biggest successes.

Music by Kenneth Morris

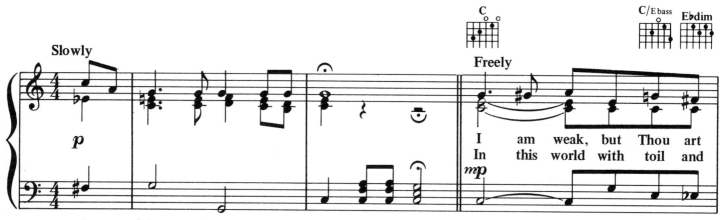

Organ pedal tacet till Chorus

CHORUS (*in tempo**)

Thee.
Thee.

Just a clos-er walk with Thee,

Grant it Je-sus is my plea,——— Dai-ly walk-ing close to

D.C. for additional verse

Thee,——— Let it be, dear Lord, let it be.

Let it be, dear Lord, let it be.

Very quietly

*Slowly, but with a double-time feeling; count 8 beats to the bar (♪ = 1 beat).

Beautiful Isle of Somewhere

Moderately

(1) Some - where the sun is shin - ing, Some - where the song - birds
(2) Some - where the day is long - er, Some - where the task is
(3) Some - where the load is lift - ed, Close by an o - pen

(1) dwell;_____ Hush, then, thy sad re - pin - ing,
(2) done;_____ Some - where thy heart is strong - er,
(3) gate;_____ Some - where the clouds are rift - ed,

Islands have always been loved by poets for their sequestered peacefulness. Islands are serene cradles, lapped round on all sides by protecting water. To a nation still torn asunder by the aftermath of the Civil War, Jessie B. Pounds' affecting metaphor, written in 1867 and set to music by John S. Fearis, was immediately soothing. Her island of Somewhere is the home of souls whose happiness is now eternal, for whom the sun of perfect light has set, and to whose ears each comforting sound is as sweet as a birdcall. Among the many admirers of "Beautiful Isle of Somewhere" was President William McKinley, whose favorite song it is said to have been. It was sung at his funeral.

Words by Jessie B. Pounds   Music by John S. Fearis

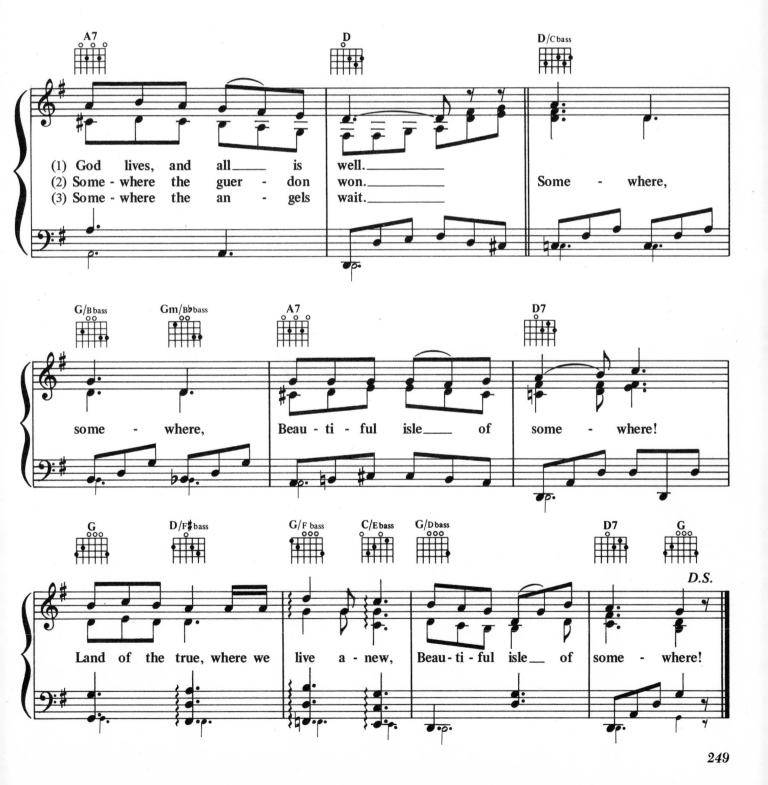

ABIDE WITH ME

Words by Henry Francis Lyte   **Music by William H. Monk**

Moderately

(1) A - bide with me, fast falls the e - ven - tide,
(2) Swift to its close fast ebbs out life's lit - tle day,

mf

The dark - ness deep - ens, Lord, with me a - bide.
Earth's joys grow dim, its glo - ries pass a - way.

(3) I need Thy presence ev'ry passing hour;
    What but Thy grace can foil the tempter's pow'r?
    Who like Thyself my guide and stay can be?
    Thro' cloud and sunshine, O abide with me!

This, perhaps the loveliest of all sunset songs, was long thought to be the dying words of its author, Henry Francis Lyte. His family maintained that he wrote it when he found, for reasons of health, he had to leave his parish in England and go to the warmer climate of southern France. (Ironically, he had always complained about being "jostled from one curacy to another.") More recent documents suggest that Lyte composed the stanzas in 1820, a quarter of a century before, after a visit to a friend who, as he lay dying, implored him ceaselessly with the phrase, "Abide with me." In any case, the pensive mood is as beautiful as it is pervasive, and the music, by William H. Monk, echoes this fragile combination. According to Monk's widow, the tune, first called "Evening," was composed in 1847 as she and her husband watched a sunset.

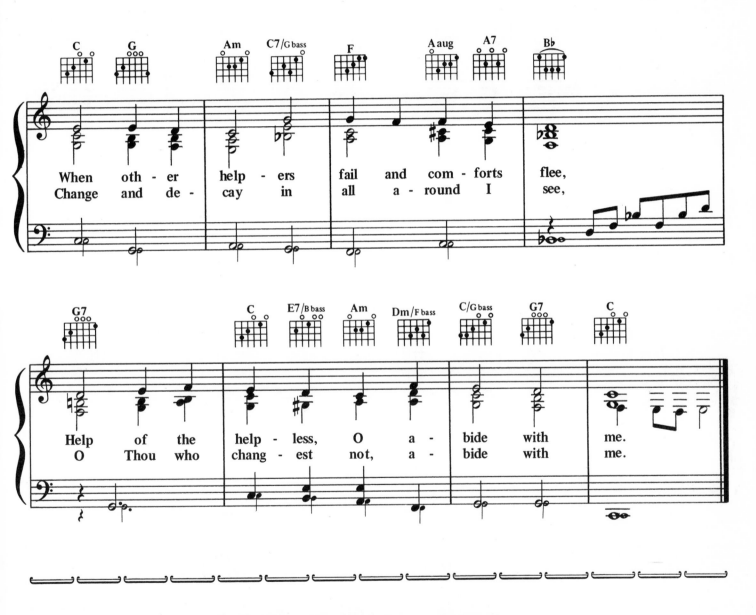

When oth- er help- ers fail and com - forts flee,
Change and de- cay in all a - round I see,
Help of the help - less, O a - bide with me.
O Thou who chang - est not, a - bide with me.

(4) Hold Thou Thy cross before my closing eyes,
Shine thro' the gloom, and point me to the skies.
Heav'n's morning breaks, and earth's vain shadows flee,
In life, in death, O Lord, abide with me!

The Lost Chord

Words by Adelaide Proctor
Music by Sir Arthur Sullivan

Sir Arthur Sullivan, who with William S. Gilbert created a fountain of light opera that is still gushing out its delights to an ever-widening audience, composed at least one serious melody — occasioned by the death of his brother Frederick—that rivals H.M.S. Pinafore and The Mikado in popularity. Sullivan's grief was all the more profound for being quiet; the only outward manifestation he allowed himself was the composition of a song, "The Lost Chord." Wherever it was heard, right from the first, it was loved. Something in the intimacy of the opening measures and the majesty of the close speaks to every heart and remains to comfort. Only 2 years after its composition, the New York Herald, saluting the English composer, who was making a visit to the United States, wrote that the song was being heard "echoing in a thousand drawing rooms." Now, a century later, it is probably one of the most treasured songs in the world.

Seat - ed one day at the or - gan, I was wea - ry and ill at
flood - ed the crim - son twi - light Like the close of an an - gel's

ease, And my fin - gers wan - der'd i - dly
psalm, And it lay on my fe - ver'd spir - it With a

253

I Need Thee Ev'ry Hour

Words by Annie Sherwood Hawks   Music by Robert Lowry

(1) I need Thee ev-'ry hour, Most gra - cious___ Lord; No

(2) I need Thee ev-'ry hour, Stay Thou near - by; No Temp-

ten - der voice like Thine, Can peace_____ af - ford.

ta - tions lose their power, When Thou___ art___ nigh.

As a 14-year-old girl, Annie Sherwood Hawks began writing bits of poetry, mostly about nature or her family, for the newspapers in upstate New York where she lived. Ten years later, in 1859, she married and moved to Brooklyn, where she joined the Hanson Place Baptist Church and soon found a new impetus for her writing. The pastor, Robert Lowry, also a writer and a musician, encouraged her poetic efforts and suggested that she concentrate particularly on hymns. Sometimes he composed the music himself, as he did in "I Need Thee Ev'ry Hour," his and Mrs. Hawks' best known hymn. It was also his idea in this case to add the refrain, "I need Thee, O I need Thee," so that the song resembled the many gospel hymns he published in collections such as Pure Gold for the Sunday School *and* Good as Gold, *a sequel.*

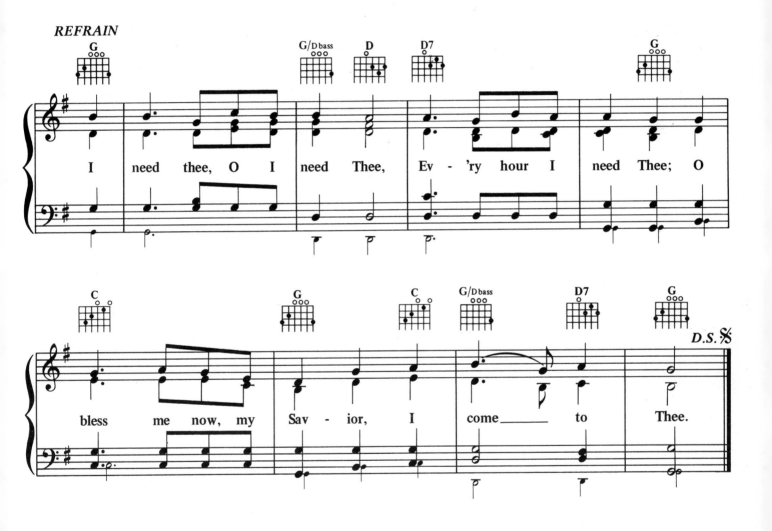

(3) I need Thee ev'ry hour,
In joy or pain;
Come quickly and abide,
Or life is vain.
Refrain

(4) I need Thee ev'ry hour,
Teach me Thy will;
And Thy rich promises
In me fulfill.
Refrain

BRAHMS' LULLABY

**Words by Karl Simrock, Translated by
Arthur Westbrook   Music by Johannes Brahms**

Johannes Brahms left several proofs of his great love for his mother. One was a sublimely beautiful section of his exalted "German Requiem," written as a special tribute after her death, which bespeaks the grandeur of his love. Another was perhaps the sweetest cradle song the world knows, which he composed the very same summer (1868). Its softly rocking rhythm and the serenity of its refrain seem to have been written for all mothers to comfort all children everywhere.

Praise God From Whom All Blessings Flow

Thomas Ken was one of the most formidable churchmen of 17th-century England. King Charles II, admiring his audacity for refusing the use of his house to Nell Gwyn, the King's mistress, rewarded him with a handsome bishopric. Bishop Ken was later tried for sedition (but acquitted) for opposing James II's Declaration of Indulgence, which was designed to promote Catholicism. He finally lost his bishopric for refusing to swear allegiance to William and Mary after the Glorious Revolution. But Bishop Ken is best remembered for his poems. One of the most famous is this hymn, "Praise God From Whom All Blessings Flow," now sung to a sturdy musical setting from the Genevan Psalter, first published in 1551.

Words by Thomas Ken

Firmly (don't drag)

Praise God, from whom all bless - ings flow; Praise Him all crea - tures here be - low; Praise Him a - bove, Ye heav'n - ly host; Praise Fa - ther, Son, and Ho - ly Ghost.

Beyond the Sunset

The well-known husband and wife team of Virgil and Blanche Kerr Brock produced "Beyond the Sunset" in their customary way; he wrote the lyrics and she the music. Both grew up in the Midwest, playing the piano, singing in church choirs, and doing solos in the camps of the great evangelistic revival leaders whose work was so influential in centers like Chatauqua and reached out to all parts of the country. Like many of the Brocks' songs ("Sing and Smile and Pray," "Keep Looking Up," and "He's a Wonderful Savior to Me," for example), "Beyond the Sunset" has a melody that, once heard, is unforgettable, and the kind of sentiments—"In that fair homeland we'll know no parting"—that only grow more beautiful with familiarity.

Words by Virgil P. Brock   Music by Blanche Kerr Brock

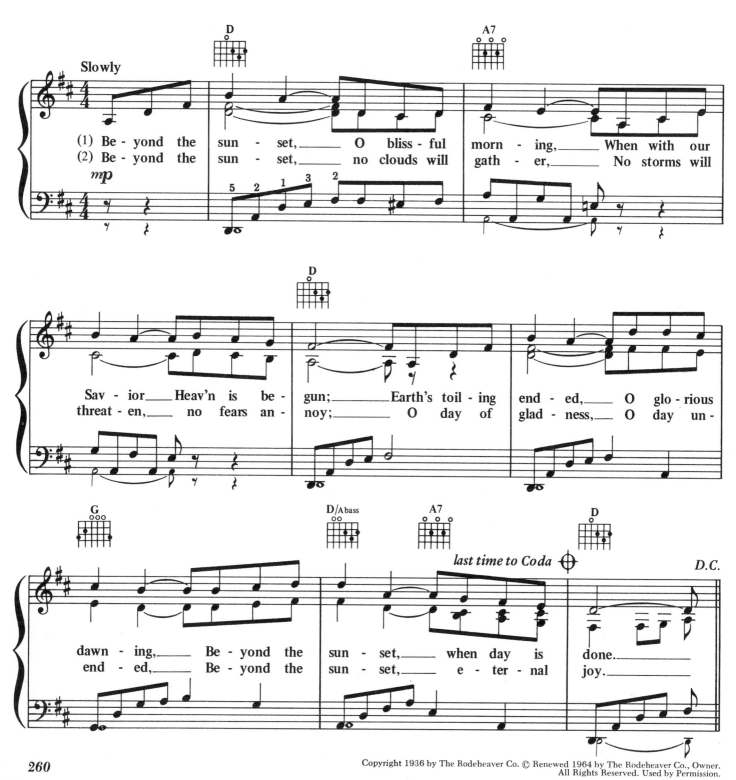

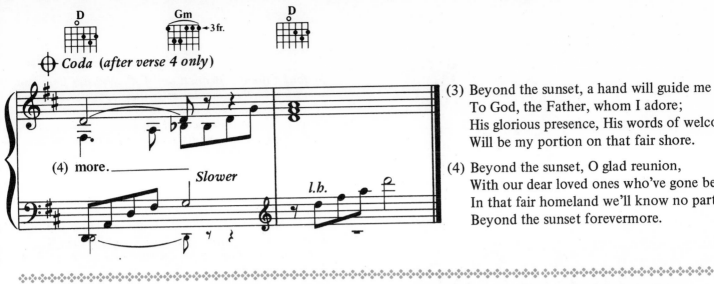

(3) Beyond the sunset, a hand will guide me
To God, the Father, whom I adore;
His glorious presence, His words of welcome,
Will be my portion on that fair shore.

(4) Beyond the sunset, O glad reunion,
With our dear loved ones who've gone before;
In that fair homeland we'll know no parting,
Beyond the sunset forevermore.

Give Us This Day

Words and Music by R. Roy Coats

R. Roy Coats produced a book of popular hymns and inspirational compositions called Golden Nuggets, *but he is best remembered for his work with a particular instrument—the saxophone. As a young man he organized, mostly in Tennessee and Mississippi, whole bands of saxophones.*

"Give us this day our dai - ly bread," Our Lord taught us to

pray._____ But make us thank - ful most of all

For Thine own self to - day. A - men.

261

In the Sweet By and By

Sanford Fillmore Bennett and J. P. Webster found so much joy in their hobby of writing songs and gospel hymns together that it nearly eclipsed their professional livelihoods as medical man and instrumentalist, respectively. They published several hundred of their own songs themselves, including "In the Sweet By and By," which has become their most famous. It appeared first in their collection of 1867 called The Signet Ring. Webster, visiting Bennett, mentioned some trifling complaint about his health but shrugged it off and said, "Everything will be all right in the sweet by and by." Bennett's imagination was struck by the words. He jotted down a few simple stanzas, and as he worked, Webster, also inspired, composed the music. Both were finished within an hour. The song was first performed that very afternoon and almost immediately became one of "the blessings that hallow our days."

Words by Sanford F. Bennett   Music by J. P. Webster

(1) way, To pre - pare us a dwell - ing place there.
(2) more, Not a sigh for the bless - ing of rest.
(3) love And the bless - ings that hal - low our days.

CHORUS

In the sweet by and by We shall meet on that beau - ti - ful

shore; In the sweet by and by We shall

meet on that beau - ti - ful shore.

(2) We shall shore.
(3) To our Slower

263

When You Come to the End of the Day

Frank Westphal, born in Chicago in 1889, organized his own dance band at an early age and played all over the American Midwest. His music avoided the popular chic so prevalent at the time. Among his own works he liked best such simple patriotic songs as "The Land We Love," "Old Soldiers Never Die," and "My Own U.S.A.," or gently swaying ballads like "When You Come to the End of the Day" (with lyrics by the immortal Gus Kahn). For the phrase, "Do you ever watch the setting sun," Westphal managed to achieve the perfect matching musical line—a slow descent in ¾ time that almost brings a vivid picture of such a sunset before our eyes. When Westphal died in 1948, the song was played at his funeral service.

Words by Gus Kahn   Music by Frank Westphal

May the Good Lord ❋ Bless ❋ and Keep You

Meredith Willson can recall vividly the Sunday school class his mother taught. "Her weekly farewell," he says, was, " 'May the good Lord bless and keep you till we meet again.' " Years later—in the early 1950's—Willson became musical director of the lavish, 90-minute radio program, The Big Show, starring Tallulah Bankhead and presenting dozens of other stars. The show was broadcast on Sunday, and one of Willson's jobs was to provide a suitable closing theme song. Harking back to his childhood and his mother's weekly farewell, he composed "May the Good Lord Bless and Keep You" in a single day. He taught the new song to Miss Bankhead who, in Willson's words, "was a smash."

Words and Music by Meredith Willson

meet a - gain. May you walk with sun - light shin - ing, and a blue - bird in ev - 'ry

tree, May there be a sil - ver lin - ing back of ev - 'ry cloud you see. Fill your

dreams with sweet to - mor - rows, nev - er mind what might have been, May the

good Lord bless and keep you till we meet a - gain, May the good Lord bless and

keep you till we meet,___ till we meet___ a - gain.___

Bless This House

Two Englishwomen, poet Helen Taylor and composer May H. Brahe, published a new hymn in 1927, which they called "Bless the House." A few years later the world-famous Irish tenor John McCormack heard their song and decided immediately to make it part of his repertoire, first suggesting that the title and corresponding lyrics be changed to the form in which we know them today. McCormack's ringing performances started the song on its way to popularity, and in 1951 its success was absolutely assured when a weekly radio program with a huge audience picked "Bless This House" as its closing theme.

Words by Helen Taylor   **Music by May H. Brahe**

Bless this house, O Lord we pray, Make it safe by night and day;

Bless these walls, so firm and stout, Keep-ing want and trou-ble out;

Note: It is very important to pay strict attention to all dynamic and tempo markings in this arrangement.

The House I Live In
(That's America to Me)

In 1933, when he received his degree in music from the University of Washington, Earl Robinson, was bursting with patriotic fervor and looking for a chance to "write music that says something." He encountered a folksong group called The Almanacs, made up of Lee Hays and Pete Seeger, composers of "If I Had a Hammer," and Woody Guthrie, who wrote "This Land Is Your Land." The trio told Robinson: "We got our stuff from the people themselves; that's where the best music and poetry can be found." Robinson was an apt pupil as is demonstrated by the gripping melody he composed for this song of brotherhood, "The House I Live In."

Words by Millard Lampell   **Music by Earl Robinson**

The house I live in, a
The place I work in, the

plot of earth, a street,   The
work - er at my side,   The

gro - cer and the butch - er and the
lit - tle town or cit - y, where my

peo - ple that I meet;   The
peo - ple lived and died;   The

chil - dren in the play - ground, the
"how - dy" and the hand - shake, the

faces that I see, All races, all re-li-gions, that's A-
air of feel-ing free, The right to speak my mind out, that's A-

mer-i-ca to me.
mer-i-ca to me.

f

The things I see a-bout me, the big things and the small, The

lit-tle cor-ner news-stand and the house a mile___ tall; The
cresc. little by little

wed-ding and the church-yard, the laugh-ter and the tears, The

America the Beautiful

Words by Katherine Lee Bates   **Music by Samuel A. Ward**

Moderately

(1) O beau - ti - ful for spa - cious skies, For am - ber waves of
(2) O beau - ti - ful for pil - grim feet, Whose stern im - pas - sioned
(3) O beau - ti - ful for pa - triot dream That sees be - yond the

mp

(1) grain, For pur - ple moun - tain maj - es - ties A -
(2) stress, A thor - ough - fare for free - dom beat A -
(3) years, Thine al - a - bas - ter ci - ties gleam, Un -

Katherine Lee Bates, a professor of English at Welles-ley College in Massachusetts, visited Pikes Peak in the summer of 1893. It was a hard wagon drive through the heat and thin air to the top, but when she attained it, the view provided an incredible feast for her New England eyes: the russet and purple mountains and the golden green valleys below, and the arch of the infinite sky above. "It was then and there," she said, "that the opening line of a poem floated into my mind—'O Beau-tiful for spacious skies . . .'!" Later she sketched out the remainder of the verse. When the poem was published, more than 60 composers offered to set the words to music. But Miss Bates chose a melody written for a hymn in 1882 by Samuel Augustus Ward. Ward's music and Professor Bates' lyrics are now happily in-separable. Once, while being honored for her work by educators and musicians, Miss Bates remarked: "It is not work to write a song; it is a great joy."

Give Me Your Tired, Your Poor

In 1876 France announced it was giving the United States a statue commemorating the American centennial. A few years later the enormous sculpture was delivered, and a few years after that the famous American journalist and philanthropist Joseph Pulitzer organized a subscription to raise money for a base to support the statue. This endeavor provided Irving Berlin with the plot for his 1949 musical hit, *Miss Liberty* (with the book by Robert E. Sherwood). In a sense the base inspired the final stirring song for the show. Berlin set to music the stanza that is inscribed on the base, which is a verse from a longer poem by Emma Lazarus called "The New Colossus."

Words From the Poem "The New Colossus" by Emma Lazarus   **Music by Irving Berlin**

GOD BLESS AMERICA

"I came here as an immigrant from Russia in 1893, and whatever success I have had as a songwriter I owe to this country." These are words from a man whose "God Bless America," one of the top patriotic songs of all times, has frequently been proposed as a new national anthem. It was introduced by Kate Smith in 1938.

When Berlin was 80, in 1968, he chose to perform "God Bless America" himself at his own birthday party on the Ed Sullivan television show. "I've tried," he said later, "to express my feelings in 'God Bless America,' a song which is not alone a song but an expression of my gratitude to the country that inspired it."

Words and Music by Irving Berlin

★★☆ Battle Hymn of the Republic ★★★

Julia Ward Howe, deeply concerned about the issues of the Civil War, decided to visit an Army camp near Washington in 1861. A song she heard there obsessed her; it was "John Brown's Body," a Methodist hymn tune to which soldiers had given more military, if hardly genteel, lyrics. Her mind caught by its rhythms, Mrs. Howe spent a sleepless night at the Willard Hotel in Washington thinking out some rhymes; the next morning she jotted down the poem that has made her name famous forever. Time has only burnished the song's glory and made it brighter. Every few years a special performance or a fresh arrangement makes us hear the inspiring words and triumphant melody as if they were once again totally new.

Words by Julia Ward Howe

280

(3) He has sounded forth the trumpet that shall never sound retreat;
He is sifting out the hearts of men before His judgment seat;
O be swift, my soul, to answer Him! be jubilant, my feet!
Our God is marching on. *Chorus*

(4) In the beauty of the lilies, Christ was born across the sea,
With a glory in His bosom that transfigures you and me;
As He died to make men holy, let us die to make men free,
While God is marching on. *Chorus*

This Land Is Your Land

In the early 1930's balladeer, poet, philosopher, and grassroots American Woody Guthrie was enthusiastic about a family of singers called The Carters, whose nasal twangs and primitive songs were about as authentic and unspoiled as one could find. Themes from two of their inimitable collections found their way—probably without his ever realizing it—into Guthrie's own "This Land Is Your Land," published in 1956. However the words and the unabashed, shore-to-shore patriotism of the song are Guthrie's own. This, his most famous composition, became virtually the national anthem of the folksong revival that began in the 1950's. Guthrie died in 1967.

Words and Music by Woody Guthrie

282

283

This Is My Country

In the late 1930's and early 1940's, when the whole world could feel murmurings of imminent war, there was a sudden surge of patriotic poems and songs, capped by a jubilant and captivating anthem to America called "This Is My Country." It was written by Don Raye and Al Jacobs, two arrangers whose music Fred Waring often programmed for his Pennsylvanians on his popular radio show. Waring introduced the song in 1940. Along with Irving Berlin's sentimental and hymnlike "God Bless America," which had been premiered just 2 years earlier, this energetic, strutting paean became a rallying cry and a source of strength for soldiers and civilians alike during World War II. It is pure patriotism at its strongest, love of country at its unabashed height.

Words and Music by Don Raye and Al Jacobs

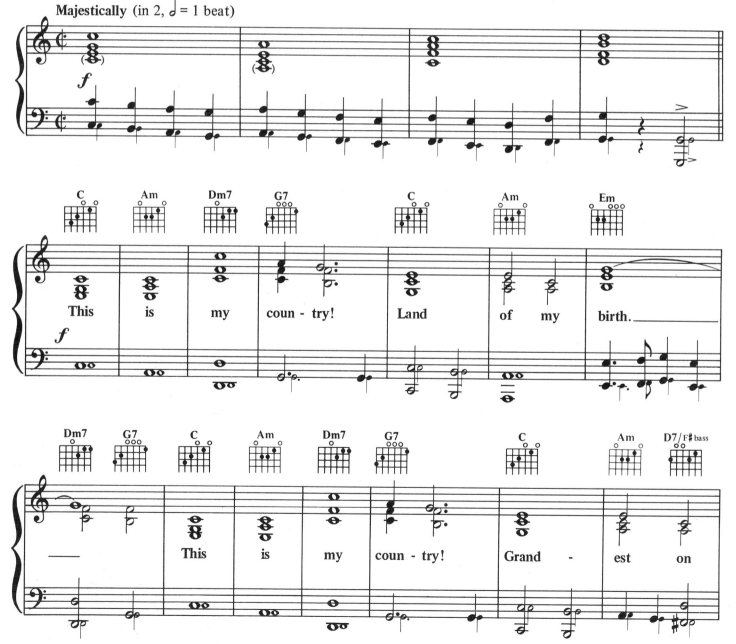

284

Earth!_____

I pledge thee my al - le -

giance, A - mer - i - ca,_____ the bold._____ For

this is my coun - try, to have

f Slower and more deliberately

and to hold!_____

(guitar tacet)

Lift Ev'ry Voice and Sing

In 1901, just 3 years before they wrote Teddy Roosevelt's Presidential campaign song, James Weldon Johnson and J. Rosamond Johnson composed a tribute to Abraham Lincoln called "Lift Ev'ry Voice and Sing." The former jotted down the words from a rocking chair on their front porch and passed them through an open window to his brother who was seated at the piano. The song was first sung at graduation exercises in the Jacksonville, Florida, high school where their mother —the first black woman in Florida's public school system—taught. Both men went on to important and varied careers—in music, theater, education, diplomacy, literature, and civil rights—and their song went on to national fame. At first the song was pasted in the backs of hymnals in a few black churches; today it is the official song of the NAACP and is often called the "national black anthem," though its stirring rhythm and words reach the hearts of whites and blacks.

Words by James Weldon Johnson   **Music by J. Rosamond Johnson**